ALSO BY YVON CHOUINARD

Let My People Go Surfing
Climbing Ice

THE
RESPONSIBLE
COMPANY

"The most important right we have
is the right to be responsible."
—*Gerald Amos*

THE
RESPONSIBLE
COMPANY

YVON
CHOUINARD
AND
VINCENT
STANLEY

PATAGONIA BOOKS | 2012

THE RESPONSIBLE COMPANY

Patagonia Books

First edition

Printed in Canada on 100 percent recycled paper

Patagonia Books, an imprint of Patagonia Inc.,
publishes a select number of titles on wilderness,
wildlife, and outdoor sports that inspire
and restore a connection to the natural world.

Project Manager: Jennifer Sullivan
Editor: Susan Bell
Designed by Barbara deWilde

Cover art, *Ash*, 56" x 56" relief print courtesy of Bryan Nash Gill,
from *Woodcut* (New York: Princeton Architectural Press, 2012).
BryanNashGill.com.

Author photos: Yvon Chouinard by Jeff Johnson,
Vincent Stanley by Tim Davis

Library of Congress Control Number: 2012934400

ISBN 978-0-980-12278-7

THE
RESPONSIBLE
COMPANY

CONTENTS

THIS BOOK IS DEDICATED TO
ALL PATAGONIA EMPLOYEES, PRESENT AND PAST

THE RESPONSIBLE COMPANY

CHAPTER 1
WHAT WE DO FOR A LIVING

W<small>E ARE ALL STILL</small> in the earliest stages of learning how what we do for a living both threatens nature and fails to meet our deepest human needs. The impoverishment of our world and the devaluing of the priceless undermine our physical and economic well-being.

Yet the depth and breadth of technological innovation of the past few decades shows that we have not lost our most useful gifts: humans are ingenious, adaptive, clever. We also have moral capacity, compassion for life, and an appetite for justice. We now need to more fully engage these gifts to make economic life more socially just and environmentally responsible, and less destructive to nature and the commons that sustain us.

This book aims to sketch, in light of our environmental crisis and economic sea change, the elements of business responsibility for our time, when everyone in business—at every level—has to deal with the unintended consequences of a 200-year-old industrial model that can no longer be sustained ecologically, socially, or financially.

The co-authors have been involved with Patagonia since its inception nearly forty years ago. But it is not the purpose of this book to retell our company's history in detail. That story may be found in Yvon's book, *Let My People Go Surfing*.

This book, though it draws on our experience at Patagonia, aims to be useful to all people who see the need for deep change in business practices and who work in companies quite unlike ours. Although we mostly address companies that make things, or like us, design things made by others, this book is germane to all businesses that offer a service or to nongovernmental organizations (NGOs) and nonprofits that want to treat their people well and reduce the environmental impact of their operations. This book is for anyone who works, not just business leaders and managers. It is also for business students and other young people who want to engage their best, deepest self in the working life that stretches ahead.

You should know that at its beginning Patagonia was meant to be not a risk-taking, environment-obsessed, navel-gazing company but an easy-to-milk cash cow. Yvon created Patagonia as an offshoot of the Chouinard Equipment Company, which made excellent mountain-climbing gear recognized as the best in the world, but very little money. Patagonia was intended to be a clean and easy company—desk jockey's work—in contrast to the ten hours a day sweat and toil of hammering out pitons with a coal-fired forge or drilling and cutting chocks from extruded aluminum. The clothing business required no expensive dies to amortize and had a much broader customer base than a few dirtbag climbers. Who knew then that cotton could be as dirty as coal?

At Chouinard Equipment we were used to a life-or-death standard of product quality: you did not sell an ice axe without checking it closely for a hairline fracture or any other fault. Although we applied the same standard to rugby shirts (they had to be thick and tough to survive the skin-shredding sport of rock climbing), we knew that seam failure was unlikely to kill anyone. Patagonia was to be our *irresponsible* company, bringing in easy money, a softer life, and enough profits to keep Chouinard Equipment in the black.

Our responsibilities as businesspeople came slowly and almost involuntarily to light while we focused on the "real" work of designing our clothes and getting them made and sold. In the chapters ahead, we'll describe a handful of moments that stunned us into consciousness (including the discovery that cotton, our most commonly used natural fiber, turned out to be the most toxic) to illustrate how one step makes the next step possible—a simple lesson but key.

{ 3 }

We can't pose Patagonia as the model of a responsible company. We don't do everything a responsible company can do, nor does anyone else we know. But we can illustrate how any group of people going about their business can come to realize their environmental and social responsibilities, then begin to act on them; how their realization is progressive: actions build on one another.

We used to think that because Patagonia grew out of a small band of climbers and surfers who have a special love for the natural world and a palpable need to be in it, feel a part of it, that we were somehow exceptional as a business. Twenty years ago, we didn't think we had much to say to the woman next to us on the plane who might wear a Chanel suit and pearls and fetch a copy of *Fortune* out of her Tod's handbag (we would have been accidentally upgraded to business class to be anywhere near her). Now, though, we can think of a number of topics we might have discussed, from design to inventory control to the implications of material shortages for long-term planning. We now know, from talking to all kinds of businesspeople, that Patagonia, if exceptional at all, is so only at the margins. As mice and men share 99 percent of their genes, so do Wal-Mart, BP, and Patagonia. Patagonia may seem different because its owners are committed to social and environmental change; and our company is privately held, not publicly traded, so we can take on greater risks. But our management requires the same sets of skills, pursues the same opportunities, and faces the same competition and constraints as any other business.

We started as climbers and surfers, so our direct engagement with nature may have allowed us to recognize the environmental crisis earlier than others and begin to act on it more quickly. But eventually the crisis would become apparent to everyone in business. Soon we would trade stories with other businesses that acted out of environmental and social concerns. In our earliest days, we talked with the founders of Ben & Jerry's, The Body Shop, and Smith & Hawken. Later, conversations with REI, The North Face, and other companies in the outdoor industry led to the creation of the Conservation Alliance, a nonprofit that protects wilderness as habitat and space for recreation.

When we finally turned a cold eye to our own wasteful and polluting industrial practices, or those done in our name by our suppliers, we sought out and found other concerned companies willing to offer advice and help. Often they were huge, and included Levi Strauss, Nike, Timberland, and The Gap. We spoke with others farther afield, like the courtly carpet-tile manufacturer Ray Anderson, founder of Interface, whose spiritual epiphany upon reading Paul Hawken's *The Ecology of Commerce* led him to become, as *The Economist* noted in his obituary, "America's greenest businessman." It turned out we were not unique in our desire to become a more responsible business.

When we wanted to improve our quality without increasing our costs, we shared notes with Jack Stack, who with other employees had

{ 4 }

bought back the failing Springfield Remanufacturing Company from International Harvester and had made it successful through innovations in participatory corporate control (i.e., listening to front-line employees) and open-book management. Jack taught us that any successful business strategy had to engage the intelligence of the people on the floor as much as of those at the top.

Along the way we've seen a tectonic shift in work culture in many businesses. During the past twenty years, Silicon Valley companies have turned old work rules on their head. Almost everyone is familiar with the free fitness rooms and free food. Fewer know that Google allows employees to spend 20 percent of their working time doing almost anything they like: We know, because some employees of Google Earth donate that time—and their technological expertise—to helping wildlands activists map migration corridors for large animals displaced by climate change and development.

We've seen the rise of specialty bakers and brewers, and of organic farms and farmers' markets, as well as the mainstreaming of what used to be called health foods. We've seen the introduction of Leadership in Energy and Environmental Design (LEED) standards revolutionize commercial construction by proving that greener building standards create healthier workspaces and that better-quality construction repays owners and investors over time.

There are many new businesses that are sensitive to their workers' needs and mindful of nature's vulnerability; and many older businesses have begun to come around. But none of us have done nearly enough.

Those who plan for the future of their businesses, in every industry, have to take into account the increasing scarcity of energy and water and their rising cost, as well as the rising cost of waste and its disposal. Every company—from Wal-Mart to the Cheese Board Collective, from BP to the makers of Fat Tire Ale, from Dow Chemical to Patagonia—is already at work, in some way, even inadvertently, to dismantle a creaky, polluting, wasteful, and increasingly expensive industrial system, and is struggling to create new, less life-draining ways to make things; we are all trying to get a new roof up over the economy before the old, sagging one caves in.

Every company faces questions from skeptical customers: Will your company's product or service hurt them or their children? Has your product hurt the workers who made it, or their community, or the ecology of the region where the product's components were drilled, mined, or farmed? Is your product worth its social and environmental cost? It may arguably have a social benefit that outweighs its cost; but everything we all do at work, unless you happen to sell organic seeds or night-soil compost, hurts the environment more than it gives back.

Your customer may not be eager to know what's wrong with your products, but if and when she finds out, she is likely to care. And she no longer has to tune into 60 *Minutes* or subscribe to *Mother Jones* to find out who's dumping chemicals or mountaintops into the local creek. Any citizen with a cell-phone camera and access to a blog can now sound the neighborly alarm. And others can spread it—and will.

This is not news to the businesspeople at work on one or more of 400 new indexes to benchmark, and advance, their social and environmental practices in the outdoor, apparel, automobile, electronics, chemical, and other industries. No one wants to feel the heat of an unfavorable spotlight. Every company should be afraid, as is Wal-Mart, of teenagers, and what they will consider environmentally acceptable or socially cool as they come into adulthood. No one under forty has ever lived in a year without an Earth Day or thought the health of an ecosystem subordinate to the whims of a corporation.

Wal-Mart woke up after a survey by McKinsey & Company jarred then-CEO Lee Scott: 54 percent of customers thought Wal-Mart "too aggressive," 82 percent expected the company to be a "role model for other businesses," and 2 to 8 percent, as many as fourteen million people, had stopped shopping at Wal-Mart altogether because they were upset by things they had heard about the company.

Some companies begin to change their ways in order to protect their reputation. Others change to reduce their cost. Still others change because they see opportunities to create new markets, whether to satisfy customers who want healthy, organic food or purchasing agents for public institutions who have to meet new environmental mandates for everything from vehicles to cafeteria napkins.

Every company faces competitors who, through their own efforts to thrive, become more adaptive, nimble, and efficient, as well as less wasteful and harmful. A company that can make environmental improvements will attract more customers. Companies that do business globally have to choose whether to adopt the toughest European standards or divide up their production and make lower-quality goods for the rest of the world. The choice they make will not go unnoticed {7} by the watchful eyes of NGOs and competitors.

Investors, especially large institutional investors like pension funds and universities, now allocate more of their portfolios to socially and environmentally responsible mutual funds, not just to pay ethical lip service or ward off demonstrations on campus. For all investors, including individuals who rely on 401(k) accounts to fund their retirement, faith in the Modern Portfolio Theory (MPT) of diversified investment to minimize risk has been sorely tested by gyrations of the past fifteen years. According to a new Harvard Business School study, socially responsible investments, which once underperformed more enticing opportunities like subprime mortgages, now over the long term outperform the market as a whole.

No company has to rely solely on its own resources to attract responsibly minded employees, customers, and investors. Every company can work with other companies, often under the auspices of a trade association, to co-develop more responsible business standards, practices, and benchmarks: then share information to help everyone reduce industrial harm and waste. That levels the playing field on which companies can then compete in good faith.

Every company that thinks it's a good guy or wants to be— Patagonia, Interface, Stonyfield Farms, etc.—has to make room in our little clubhouse for old villains who now don a white hat for at least part of the working day. They are legion. Nike, stung by public disgust over child labor in its contract factories, has become a global leader in the effort to improve workplace conditions throughout the supply chain and create at least minimally fair labor practices around the world.

After being criticized for polluting groundwater and sucking wells dry in India, Coca-Cola has committed to return its wastewater to the environment clean enough "to support aquatic life and agriculture."

Dow Chemical, former maker of napalm, has committed to finding alternatives to petroleum as a source for its chemicals. Dow has recently teamed with The Nature Conservancy on a five-year, $10-million exploratory project to develop methodologies that can assign dollar values to ecosystems. These new tools will allow Dow to evaluate the ecological costs of every business decision it makes. Moreover, Dow was awarded an A+ from the Global Reporting Initiative (GRI) for its 2010 Annual Sustainability Report. Both Coca-Cola and Dow have teamed with Kellogg's, DuPont, and others to develop "material-neutral" packaging (packaging is responsible for a third of all waste generated).

And Wal-Mart, the world's largest company, formerly committed to an exclusive strategy of low prices, regardless of environmental cost, has committed to use 100 percent renewable energy, create zero waste, and to "sell products that sustain our resources and environment."

Consumers, both individual and institutional, have become and will continue to be more demanding. Individual consumers are famously powerful for controlling two-thirds of the U. S. economy. For local, state, and national governments and public institutions, who all buy "in bulk," the Prius is succeeding the late Crown Victoria as the emblematic tax-exempt fleet vehicle (although the NYPD prefers the hybrid Nissan Altima).

Whole industries are changing. The conservative but troubled U.S. dairy industry is now engaged in large-scale projects to increase the productivity and shelf life of milk without resorting to destructive factory-farm practices; to change cattle feed to reduce methane "burps" (a significant contributor to greenhouse gases); and to harvest cow patties for use as organic fertilizer.

The commercial construction industry ten years ago was no bastion of green: its old, fixed-budget business model, based on the low bid, drove down quality at every stage of design and construction. Every builder had requirements to build to code but no incentives to build in resource-saving systems that might cut the building owner's cost in {9} the long run but not the short. Enter the LEED certification system for building to energy-efficient standards with less environmental harm. At the time it was introduced in 2000, only 635 buildings worldwide could comply. As of 2012, more than 40,000 LEED-certified projects have been built or are in the works.

LEED has educated building owners and managers to the long-term high cost of cheap heating and air conditioning (and of cleaning a building with high levels of indoor pollution), as well as to the savings inherent in new materials and design. An initial 2 percent increase in the cost of a new LEED-certified project incurs savings of ten times that amount over the life of the building. A LEED retrofit saves owners an annual 90 cents a square foot; they make their investment back in two years. LEED is becoming the standard for commercial properties and, in the process, changing the urban landscape. In big cities, for instance, look for more roofs planted with shrubs and herbs, which insulate, filter the air, reduce heating and cooling needs, and provide a garden haven for workers taking a break. Look for more of the kind of low-income housing built by developer Jonathan Rose, with more under-the-roof residential services and a lot more light: the gym of his new South Bronx project is located not in the basement but on the top floor.

Our own outdoor industry is changing as well. Its trade group, the Outdoor Industry Association (OIA), is developing an assessment tool called the Eco Index, for use by manufacturers to measure the social and environmental impact of every one of their products. Patagonia's Jill Dumain has been part of a working group of twenty companies that for two years met weekly by conference call to develop the relevant criteria. They benefited from participation by Nike, which had invested seven years of work and $6 million to create its Environmental Apparel Design Tool (which, for internal use, grades the impact of the company's products as bronze, silver, or gold).

{10}   The Eco Index measures impacts of manufacturing, packaging, and shipping, as well as customer care and use, recycled content, and recyclability. It allows a company to manage its entire supply chain to improve water use and quality, lower greenhouse gas emissions, and reduce toxic chemical use and waste, as well as monitor and improve pay and working conditions on the mill or factory floor.

The OIA group decided to adopt a policy of full transparency and created an advisory council that voted on all decisions. OIA also hired a consultancy firm called Zero Waste Alliance to form a collaborative framework and methodology that would work for a broad range of participating companies—some small, others quite large (among them REI and Timberland, in addition to Nike).

OIA's Eco Index council is now at work on the second stage, which will allow more than 100 companies to provide open-source tools to benchmark their practices and measure improvements through their business reporting systems. Our hope is that within five years the Eco Index will become consumer-facing (as is Berkeley professor Dara

O'Rourke's Good Guide rating system), so that a customer can scan a Quick Response (QR) code on a pair of jeans to see ratings of that product's social and environmental impact.

OIA has made the Eco Index both transparent and scaleable. As a result, the much larger Sustainable Apparel Coalition, whose members produce more than 30 percent of the clothing and footwear sold globally, will benefit from the OIA's work, shaving much time from the development of its own assessment tool.

Patagonia owes its role in the larger coalition to our relationship with Wal-Mart over the past several years. When their executives first approached us to learn more about our environmental practices, we were, from the owners to the rank and file, skeptical and bemused. How could we help them or they help us, when our two companies were so vastly different? There was the question of scale: we grossed $400 million a year, while they grossed $400 billion. There was the question of {11} business culture: Southern California versus rural Arkansas; high quality and strong aesthetics versus rock-bottom prices and pallet racks. There was the question of values. We knew ours; what did Wal-Mart value?

By the time they approached us, in 2008, Wal-Mart had gone through a gradual environmental awakening. Shaken by its declining reputation, and a historic volume of lawsuits aimed at a single company, Wal-Mart at first adopted some basic environmental improvements of the sort corporations usually have their PR departments tout to the press. But removing excess packaging from deodorant sticks, concentrating laundry detergent in small bottles, and installing auxiliary power units in their trucks to reduce idling time turned out to save them millions of dollars. The more material they shaved from packaging, the less energy they used, the more money they made. The more carbon they removed from their operations, the less money they wasted. The word "sustainable," at first the province of the PR staff, became a business by-word.

Wal-Mart's currently low-idling truck fleet is the world's largest. If Wal-Mart were an economy, it would be bigger than Switzerland. Because its material needs—for operations but especially for products—are so great, and because it runs stores around the world, in China, India, and Brazil, as well as in Europe, Wal-Mart is in a position to understand the resource restraints to be faced over the next decade. The company understands how essential it is to reduce its environmental impact if it is to continue to do business on a habitable planet.

Patagonia's talks with Wal-Mart led to a shared David and Goliath enterprise. Yvon and John Fleming, Wal-Mart's Chief Merchandising Officer, co-signed an invitation written on joint letterhead to attend the "21st Century Apparel Leadership Consortium" to be held in New York three months hence. They sent it to sixteen of the world's largest apparel companies. One sentence on the invitation, printed in boldface, read like the crack of a ruler on a wrist:

> During the course of one half day session, we expect to achieve consensus on the need for a universally accepted approach for measuring apparel sector sustainability, and to establish a strategy for ongoing collaboration to create and implement that standard.

The invitation's final sentences, printed in italic, laid out its raison d'être:

> *Creating a sustainability standard will improve the welfare of our workers, communities, consumers, and environment far more effectively than the fragmented, incremental approaches that characterize existing efforts. Together we are better. We hope you will join us.*

Join us they did. The invitees, during their meeting in New York, agreed to become the Sustainable Apparel Coalition. The coalition members, working by consensus, drew on the work of OIA's Eco Index to define its social and environmental benchmarks. The Coalition has now launched into development of an open-source assessment tool to be shared by participants. It is our hope that this index, like OIA's, can be converted eventually into a consumer-facing rating that will allow a customer to hold a smart phone to a QR code to read an individual rating—and compare the impact of one pair of jeans to another.

Similar efforts are underway in other industries, with over 400 indexes in effect or being considered that measure the impacts of everything from appliances (Energy Star ratings) to electronics (EPEAT) to automobiles. It's too early to tell, but these indexes could create a revolution in the way we buy: they certainly give us the information we need to be good citizens as well as informed buyers.

Every company has business partners—suppliers, dealers—with a stake in its success. These partners have also begun to adopt and develop, voluntarily or not, a more responsible business model for their own companies. Companies, suppliers, and retailers all need to help each other. As your company is responsible for everything done in its name, so are your partners responsible for your part of their social and ecological footprint. As Patagonia is responsible for the labor practices of Maxport, the factory in Hanoi that sews our Super Alpine Jacket, so REI is responsible for the environmental footprint of the Patagonia jackets it sells in its stores. How so? REI can't tell Patagonia how to make jackets, but it doesn't have to buy from us either. If it cares about reducing the environmental footprint of the jackets sold on its floor, REI can influence us to improve our practices or buy from someone else who will. And they should. As Wal-Mart has discovered, 90 percent of a product's environmental impact is determined at the design stage; it is the designer in Los Angeles who determines most of the harm to be done in Guangdong.

Every company now has to work to win the minds and hearts of its employees; to earn their trust, loyalty, and commitment, and to engage their intelligence to help figure out, before the old economy caves, how to put up that new roof (built out of renewable or recycled materials, to LEED standards, with a garden to reduce energy costs). To

{ 13 }

earn employee commitment and trust begs more of a company than providing competitive pay and benefits and enacting humane employment policies. Employees who grew up in the 1980s or later view it as their birthright to make the best use of their intelligence and creativity, not always for the highest pay.

Not everyone can satisfy his heart's desire working for your company, but everyone does want to feel useful at or, better yet, enlivened by what they do all day long. No one wants to be ashamed to name the company he works for. No one wants to leave her values at home when she leaves for work in the morning.

People will argue over what makes the world a better place to live (and for whom), and over what each of us would like to see more and less of in the world. It is hard to imagine anyone rejoicing over the generally accepted landscape of only a decade ago: a suburban monoculture of tilt-up malls, cracker-crumb housing, pandemic obesity, cheap distractions, and expensive services—all at the expense of nature and not much good for us as people who are part of nature. It's as though we'd handed Satan a hard hat and asked him to refashion our earth according to his plan.

A word about a word we've chosen to use as little as possible: *sustainability*. It's a legitimate term that calls us not to take more from nature than we can give back. But we do take back more than we give, we do harm nature more than we help it. We have no business applying the word sustainable to business activity until we learn to house, feed, clothe and enjoy ourselves—and fuel the effort—without interfering with nature's capacity to regenerate itself and support a rich variety of life.

We are a long, long way from doing sustainable business on a planet that now numbers seven billion human beings, including growing, appetitive (though often socially and environmentally conscious) middle classes emerging in China, India, Mexico, Brazil, and Russia. Everything we make does some damage. To produce enough gold to make a wedding band, for instance, generates 20 tons of mine waste. Closer to home: a Patagonia polo shirt is made of organic cotton from an irrigated field, whose cultivation requires nearly 2,700 liters of water, enough to meet the daily needs (three glasses a day) of 900 people. Each polo shirt, in its journey from the cotton field to our Reno warehouse, generates nearly 21 pounds of carbon dioxide, 30 times the weight of the finished product. Along the line, it generates three times its weight in waste.

No human economic activity is yet sustainable.

Twenty years ago, we at Patagonia felt compelled to include in our mission statement an industrial equivalent of the Hippocratic oath, "cause no unnecessary harm." There are degrees of harm. Our {15} polo shirt harms less than one made of chemical-intensive, conventionally farmed cotton, which may be no cleaner than coal. Our polo would be more sustainable if it were made, as are our jeans, from less thirsty, dry-farmed cotton. But even that polo would take its toll on the natural world, through its use of energy, its carbon emissions, and its waste scrap.

Still, it makes a difference to do less harm, and lessening harm makes it possible to begin to imagine restorative and even, through biomimicry, regenerative practices for the future. It makes a difference, where harm is done on an industrial scale, to make improvements on an industrial scale. It makes a difference for businesses, as well as consumers, to use fewer materials and less energy and water, and generate less waste. To make the difference we need to restore the planet to health, or to allow the planet to restore itself to health, we need to make big changes and make them fast. But it would irresponsible not to pursue every improvement, to take action, where we can.

Many companies are doing something to behave more responsibly to the earth and the commons. And every company that learns to take a responsible step without faltering gains confidence to take the next. "Responsible" seems to us the apt, more modest, word to use while we walk the path that, we hope, leads to a place where business takes no more from nature than what it can replace.

CHAPTER 2

WHAT CRISIS?

THE PHILOSOPHER Alfred North Whitehead described how we experience nature's "creative advance" as perpetual novelty. But nature generates its changes at a much slower pace than we now allow her and in more complex ways than we can easily recognize. We need to be more aware of what we do to the planet, do much less harm—and do it far more slowly.

We harm nature by what we add to it, how we alter it, and what we take away. We have added a number of chemicals that nature didn't have to absorb before the nineteenth century, and that we didn't have to deal with as health issues. The EPA identified 62,000 industrial chemicals in 1979, without screening or proscribing their use. Only a few hundred have even been tested. You carry in your own body traces of 200 chemicals unknown to your ancestors, some of them toxic in large amounts, others slow-acting carcinogens in small amounts. And a chemical present in your blood might have no affect on its own, but prove dangerous in combination with another. Untested interactions among the various chemicals released into nature can form up to three billion combinations.

Because we know so little, it is difficult to track our diseases back to their environmental source. Certain diseases have become prevalent in affluent countries at much higher rates than in the less developed world, and they may reflect a reduced physical resilience. These include inflammatory autoimmune disorders like asthma, allergies, lupus, and multiple sclerosis. Nonsmokers who reach middle age can now expect to have levels of chronic obstructive pulmonary disease (COPD), a precursor to emphysema, equal to that of smokers. Breast cancer rates for women have tripled during the past thirty years, and only 5 to 10 percent of breast cancers are considered hereditary.

Scientists are slow to link specific cancers to specific environmental causes, such as high-voltage wires, PCBs in the river, your cell phone. Few cancer catalysts have been studied as closely or confirmed as positively as cigarette smoke. But some environmentally caused illnesses can be traced: mercury poisoning, for instance, has been proven to result from eating too many large predatory fish, such as tuna and swordfish.

We have added significantly, through runoff from sewage and fertilizer, to the nitrogen and phosphorus in the water supply; the extra nutrients create algae blooms that choke off oxygen and kill fish. Half of the lakes in Asia, Europe, and North America suffer from this process, called eutrophication, as does much of the Gulf of Mexico.

We have altered nature.

The atmospheric concentration of carbon dioxide, up by 19 percent since 1959, has now reached its highest level in 600,000 years and continues to grow, making hot air hotter, cold air colder, and increasing the ferocity of storms. Arctic winter ice decreases 9 percent each decade, and every winter more of western Antarctica's ice shelves calve into the ocean. The Larsen B Ice Shelf alone was the size of Rhode Island and took only 35 days to collapse.

We have borrowed from nature what we can't pay back.

In 1960, humanity consumed about half of the planet's potential resource capacity. By 1987, we exceeded it. Twenty-five years later we are using the resource capacity of one and a half planets, though the pattern of consumption is unequal. Europe, proportionate to its population, consumes the equivalent resources of three planets; North Americans, seven. The consumers are unevenly distributed, and so is the consumption, though China and India, the world's most populous countries, now have sizeable, growing, appetitive middle classes.

Biologists agree that we're in the midst of the planet's sixth ex- {19} tinction crisis (the fifth was that of the dinosaurs). A 2009 study in *Nature* named biodiversity as the "planetary boundary" that humans have violated more than any other, among nine identified "Earth-system processes and associated thresholds, which, if crossed, could generate unacceptable environmental change." Their proposed threshold for extinction was ten species per million per year. We are losing species now at the rate of 100 per million per year, or 1,000 times (not a typo) the normal rate. Thirty percent of amphibians and 21 percent of mammals are among the most imminently vulnerable, including the polar bear, rhinoceros, tiger, giraffe, and gorilla. Twelve percent of bird species are threatened with extinction, as are 73 percent of flowering plants, 27 percent of corals, and 50 percent of fungi and protists.

Water withdrawals from lakes and rivers have doubled since 1960. As more of the earth's major rivers—on which huge populations depend—fail to reach the sea, the ocean's coastal eutrophic, or dead, zones expand. The dammed Colorado River is now rarely allowed to flow into the Gulf of Mexico, and its former delta is a toxic swamp. By 2025, no Chinese river will meet the ocean all year long, which will devastate wetlands, and decimate bird- and fishlife. China's rivers will no longer be lifelines for her people.

Worldwide, wetlands diminish and disappear year by year, as do coral reefs and mangroves; major fisheries are collapsing. Loss of rainforest continues in poorer countries. Conventional plowing and planting without crop rotation has led to significant loss of topsoil—at the rate of one inch a year in the American Midwest. It takes 500 years for an inch of topsoil to form naturally.

The human consequences of ecological overreach are magnified in poor countries and in countries like China and India, which have large poor populations: shrinking resources only aggravate the basic challenges of inadequate food, water and sanitation.

In short, the world is becoming a desert. Globalization, a manmade but not humanly controlled process, is largely responsible for the current speed at which life turns to sand. Globalization moves with great speed to identify, then harvest resources for human needs but crawls slowly to repair the devastation it has left in its wake. It is fast but stupid, brutal, and imprecise; to cull a tree, it takes out a forest.

Those who watch the forest be cut and raise their voice against it cannot be heard when the company that did the cutting does not belong to the community. And there is little community representatives can do. When local politics becomes subservient to distant economic power, the concept of citizenship, of its duties and possibilities, loses its meaning. The human commons loses its value; it too becomes desert.

Because Yvon has his roots in climbing and surfing, as does our company, we can't leave undiscussed the loss of wilderness or wildness, which is as much a spiritual concept as a definition of place. By naturalist Margaret Murie's definition, wilderness is where the hand of man does not linger.

As men and women we are part of nature. If we were to have no experience of wild nature, or no way to know of it, we would lose entirely our sense of human scale. We derive our sense of awe from our ability to feel nature's force. We better know ourselves when we come face to face with the magnificence of the unknown. Emerson, Thoreau, and other transcendentalists learned and taught these lessons in New England in the 1830s through 1860s. They showed us that we can learn directly from nature about who we are and how to live.

After an accident left him sightless in a darkened room for eight months, John Muir, a native of Scotland, began his long walking journeys, first from Indiana to Florida, then famously to Yosemite. During his wandering years, Muir carried a tin cup, a handful of tea, a loaf of bread, and a copy of Emerson. (The two men were to meet one day in 1871 in Yosemite). Muir's writings on the geology and botany of the Sierras gained him fame, respect, and economic independence. Perhaps his greatest achievement was to persuade Teddy Roosevelt to abandon the comforts of Yosemite's government camp and go off with him to sleep in bedrolls directly under the stars. That night might be regarded as the birth of the conservation movement: Muir talked Roosevelt into creating Yosemite National Park.

It might surprise some to know that, in 1972, Roosevelt's political descendant Richard Nixon, on signing the Endangered Species Act, said:

> This is the environmental awakening. It marks a new sensitivity of the American spirit and a new maturity of American public life. It is working a revolution in values, as commitment to responsible partnership with nature replaces cavalier assumptions that we can play God with our surroundings and survive. It is leading to broad reforms in action, as individuals, corporations, government, and civic groups mobilize to conserve resources, to control pollution,

to anticipate and prevent emerging environmental problems, to manage the land more wisely, and to preserve wilderness.

If the United States is the birthplace of conservation, of the very idea of wilderness as its own value, of nature as a teacher, we have not kept stride with the rest of the world. Forty years after Nixon gave that speech, we are still the leading practitioners of the kind of high-growth, material-intensive capitalism that is to blame for the destruction of nature. The respected Environmental Performance Index (EPI) in 2010 ranked the world's five top countries as Iceland, Switzerland, Costa Rica, Sweden, and Norway. Germany, the U.K., France, and Japan are all in the top twenty. The U.S. has fallen to the sixty-first position.

This decline reflects Americans' growing environmental apathy. In a 2011 poll, Pew Research Center reported that only 40 percent of Americans considered protecting the environment a high priority, down from 63 percent ten years earlier.

Will this continue? In the 1960 book *Growing Up Absurd: Problems of Youth in the Organized System*, an analysis of juvenile delinquency in an overorganized world, Paul Goodman predicted the youth movement that would rise up in the decade that followed. The civil rights and women's rights movements also arose in response to conditions that looked unshakably stable and hegemonic at the time.

Any situation keenly out of balance eventually reveals itself to large numbers of people as absurd. So it will be with our own current social and environmental disequilibrium. The authors hope that those born in the 1980s and coming into their own now will, all their lives, pursue meaningful work and do the right thing, which is to say be responsible to other people and to nature. The authors hope they reject the official story told by governments and corporations that a healthy economy relies on the suppression of social, ecological, and individual health.

It's a competitive world: Will Iceland win?

CHAPTER 3

THE RESPONSIBLE COMPANY IN OUR TIME

THAT MANY COMPANIES now act on some recently recognized responsibilities to nature and the commons does not mean that they are delighted to do so. Nor does it mean that a new, happier age of more responsible capitalism is at hand. Nothing is certain, except that the shift to more conscious, cooperative business practices will be hard, and that whatever you do, for good or ill, will matter, wherever you work.

How is a company responsible? Should it profit its shareholders, provide for the well-being of its employees, make excellent products, be a good force in the community, and protect nature? We think that a responsible company bears all these obligations. But getting into the details of how business might deal with the environmental crisis and social storms we face, it would help to better understand how a company's responsibilities differ today from 50 or 150 years ago.

The responsible company of 1860 was one that paid a return to its shareholders, honored its commitments, and kept honest books. A hundred years later the picture had become far more complex. In 1860, only 5 percent of all work was done by machine; 95 percent was done by humans and animals. By 1960, the figure reversed; 95 percent of all work was performed by machines. It would take, if it were possible, the muscle power of 700,000 people to power the flight of a jet. Machines made us capable of doing far more work than we and our animals could ever have done on our own.

In the century between 1860 and 1960, limited liability for corporations became law in order to protect shareholders and officers from imprisonment or personal bankruptcy when their companies committed damage or fraud or failed to pay their bills. But companies took on new obligations to workers as well, thanks to the growing legitimacy and power of unions and progressive political movements in industrial countries. Corporations became liable for the health and safety of the workplace. Laws enacted, if not always enforced, during the late nineteenth and early twentieth centuries limited working hours, particularly for women and children, in the U.S. and Europe, and later throughout most the world.

The big, responsible company of 1960 (in the U.S., examples included IBM, 3M, Bell & Howell, Cummins Engine, Johnson & Johnson) was rich and international, and going global. It kept honest books, hated to bribe officials, and paid its people decently (more decently its men, the better to support nonworking wives and children). It maintained substantial training and education programs and promoted from within; operated programs to increase safety in the workplace; and supported community hospitals, schools, and nonprofessional sports activities.

The big, responsible company in those days had a fixed and clear hierarchy; men were at the top and, in the U.S. and Europe, were white. The management philosophy in such a company derived from the West's earliest models for organizing large numbers of people through command and control: the military and the Roman Catholic Church, with new contributions from manufacturer Henry Ford and efficiency consultant Frederick Winslow Taylor. As they do now, the company's top executives took time out from their careers to serve in government. The company's board members also might have served on the boards of its major suppliers, customers, and banks. The company had some-times adversarial, sometimes cooperative relationships with its unions.

The standard of living for less well-educated, lower-salaried and wage-earning employees was higher than now, relative to their bosses, and a substantial number of employees could look forward confidently to a company pension as well as a check from Social Security or, in other countries, its equivalent. A big company was likely to be indus-trial, not financial; U.S. commercial banks, after New Deal reforms, could not operate across state lines, own nonbanking operations, or combine with investment banks. Big business was smaller and not as rich or powerful as now. The Dow Jones average on the last day of 1960 stood at 615.

Over the past fifty years, big business faced new regulations to prevent discrimination on the basis of race, gender, or age. In the U.S., Europe, and Japan, new environmental laws restricted air and water pollution. Technology advanced rapidly, which increased productivity, put an end to many kinds of jobs, and made many workers redundant. In the U.S., according to one researcher, five out of six lost manufactur-ing jobs could be attributed to increased productivity (with the remain-ing one out of six jobs lost to offshoring and other causes).

While the Dow grew from 1,000 in 1982 to 14,000 in 2007, this fabulous twenty-five year increase in wealth rewarded the top 10 per-

{ 25 }

cent of earners far more than the middle class. This was especially true in the U.S. and Britain. Although middle-class real earnings did not grow, net worth did for those with 401(k) accounts and real estate holdings. As incomes plateaued, the two-worker family became the norm, though the two-parent family became less so. Social safety nets began to fray throughout the most industrially advanced countries, especially in Europe and Japan, as fewer workers paid taxes to support a growing number of retirees.

As noted in the previous chapter, increased economic activity has come with incredible environmental cost, in loss of biodiversity, global deforestation, ocean pollution, and desertification. By the most visible measures—cleanliness of the air and water—the environment has improved in our country since the passage of major environmental laws in the 1970s. Angelenos can now see the San Gabriel Mountains on a summer day. The Cuyahoga River no longer catches fire. Anadromous fish return to the Hudson and Kennebec Rivers (though you are warned not to eat them).

{ 26 }

But the less visible, less stinky problems have grown worse in the form of greenhouse gases and increased carbon dioxide levels, the overfishing of increasingly acidified oceans and loss of coral that supports marine life, the drawing down of fossil-water aquifers that will take centuries to replenish, and in the failure of rivers—in Asia, life-lines for the population—to meet the sea. More than a billion people now live in areas threatened by desertification.

As of this writing, two-thirds of the U.S. economy relies on consumer spending. Editorial pundits from the center left of the The New York Times to the hard right of The Wall Street Journal pay obeisance to the god of consumer spending and its gospel of 3 percent minimum growth. This cannot be sustained. Poke your nose into any store in the mall and look around. Much of what we produce to sell to each other to earn our living is crap, either ever more luxurious, specialized goods like electronic temple massagers and personal oxygen bars, or cheap salty junk food and disposable clothing. Every piece of crap, because it was manufactured, contains within it something of the priceless: applied human intelligence, for one, natural capital for another—something taken from the forest or a river or the soil that cannot be replaced faster than we deplete it. We're wasting our brains *and* our only world on the design, production, and consumption of things we don't need and that aren't good for us.

Everything manufactured comes with a cost that exceeds its price.

Because resources continue to grow scarcer, while the world population still grows and becomes more urban, and consumes more, it seems to us that the days left to the consumer society as we know it are few in number. We are in transition to a post-consumerist society, and toward the recovery of our collective senses—of time, of public space, of proportion.

In a post-consumerist world, goods are likely to become more expensive, to reflect their true social and environmental cost, prompting us to shop less as a form of entertainment. That's not so bad. We'll be able to recover time for satisfying pleasures that derive from pursuing our deepest interests; we'll have more time with our friends and family, and more time for meaningful work.

Of course, there are other, more dystopian possibilities for an economy in which fewer and fewer people make more and more things until we run out of resources to make them and customers with enough money to buy them. Manufacturing has seen an astonishing gain in productivity (output per worker) during the past fifty years; not so the service sector now responsible for most employment. Increasingly, companies seek, when not sending jobs offshore, to ratchet up productivity through the introduction of automated systems that make nonmanufacturing jobs more factorylike (e.g., counting calls per hour and sales per call in service centers). Pressures for a more intensive, and longer, workday for white-collar jobs are likely to increase until employees resist, or workforce-squeezing companies begin to lose business to more humanly responsive companies due to poor customer service. More people, especially those without advanced, specialized education, are likely to suffer longer periods of unemployment, and hard falls through the frayed social net. It doesn't take total social and environmental breakdown to create conditions none of us would wish on our children and grandchildren.

Dystopia is not inevitable. But it will take all the intelligence and navigational skill we can muster to collectively rebuild the ship as we sail it. It will require all the heart we have in us to care for each other as we move from an economy that worked well for many of us—and for some of us splendidly— to one where no twelve-year-old works a sewing machine and lives on a bowl of rice a day, and where no Asian river flows to the sea dyed indigo, as a waste product from jeans.

Companies, large and small, will be useful to a post-consumerist society. We will continue to need food, clothing, and shelter, as well as fun and games, and to organize ourselves to provide it. We will need energy to stay warm in cold weather and cool in hot. But we are beginning to understand the true cost—human, ecological, economic—of everything we make. We need to make less, and whatever we make should be of high quality and long-lasting to better offset its social and environmental price.

In this light, a responsible company owes a return not only to stockholders but to something that has come to be called stakeholders, entities dependent on or beholden to the company, but also on which the company depends. In addition to stockholders, there are four key stakeholders: employees, customers, communities, and nature.

Stockholders still get first dibs and last, but their return relies on the cooperative productivity of the other groups.

The responsible company owes its *employees* light-handed, attentive management; openness about the numbers; encouragement to co-operate, across divisional lines when necessary, and to continuously improve processes; freedom to organize workflow with minimal delays or interference from higher-ups; and a penalty-free whistle to blow against wrongdoing.

The responsible company owes its *customers* safe, high-quality products and services; this applies to both basics and high-end goods. Goods should be well made, durable, and easily repaired. Whatever comes to the end of its useful life needs to be recycled or repurposed into something new. Marketing claims, especially those of health and environmental benefits, should be made responsibly.

The *community* includes suppliers, who have now become critical to reducing the social and environmental impacts of products. It is challenging for companies, with subcontracting so prevalent, to know, much less understand, their supply chain and its workings. But to know who does what and where enables a company to work with its suppliers more intelligently and productively—and to improve the working conditions and environmental stewardship that underlie its products.

Community also includes, of course, locality. Your company needs to take responsibility for wherever your people gather for work, including satellite locations where you have stores, warehouses, or factories. Obligation to the community includes paying a fair share of taxes and a healthy dose of philanthropy, in money and in-kind contributions of product or services. Many companies now allow their local units a say in local giving.

Community also includes trade associations, nongovernmental organizations (NGOs), standards-setting organizations, nonprofits, and

{ 29 }

other citizens' organizations that may have an interest or something to say about what your company does. Advocacy groups like Greenpeace and PETA may confront you about your practices, as may individual citizen activists through social media like Facebook and Twitter. Friendly or not, those who engage with you are part of your community in its broadest sense and deserve your attention.

Nature decides our fate but has no voice of her own, or not one that we can hear. We can't sit with her at the table and ask her what she needs to get her work done or what she cares about most. In the face of nature's silence, we have to honor the Precautionary Principle, now embedded into law in the European Union and other countries, that in the absence of scientific certainty, the burden of proof that a new product or technology is safe now falls on business. The Precautionary Principle requires us to reverse our habit, prevalent since the Industrial Revolution, to act now and deal with the consequences later.

Here are the key issues that face the responsible company in relation to its stakeholders during the next fifty years.

Stockholders: Accounting will become more complex. As ever, companies will do whatever they have to do to maintain financial health, cut the owners their checks, and meet payroll. Increasingly, however, companies will also have to measure and assign value to our social and environmental impacts or face the cruel surprise of a sudden rise in the price of carbon or drop in the availability of fresh water. As noted, The Nature Conservancy is working with Dow Chemical to assign value to what ecosystems contribute to the economy. In 2011, moreover, Puma commissioned PriceWaterhouseCoopers to help develop an "Environmental Profit and Loss" statement to account for the full impact of the brand on ecosystems. The consultancy firm hopes to create a model robust enough to be adopted by other companies.

Governments are also changing what they count. The United Nations has endorsed the principles of the "triple bottom line," or 3P (profit, people, planet), for government accounting. In 2010, Robert Zoellick, president of the World Bank, announced a major project to work with emerging and developing countries to quantify their natural capital, roughly estimated at a value of $44 trillion worldwide.

Public companies that work hard and effectively to improve their social and environmental performance will need to be protected by new laws that forbid attack by minority stockholders, who in most jurisdictions have the right to sue a company for investing in social and environmental performance at the short-term expense of stock value. At present, environmental and social improvements may be scrapped easily when a company, public or private, is sold or inherited. Several states, including California, have created a new legal class called the "benefit corporation" that allows companies to have a social or environmental mission written into their charter. Benefit-corporation status also gives a company the legal right to pursue high social and environmental standards that can benefit the company in the long term but reduce short-term earnings. An organization called B Labs grants "B Corporation" accreditation to companies that meet its standards as well as works to expand legal recognition.

Employees: There has been a fifty-year trend toward automation, moving jobs offshore, improvement in wages in developing countries, and a flattening of wages in advanced countries. The next fifty years will be marked by pressure to restore the living wage. It was assumed as late as the 1960s that the annual pay of one wage earner (usually male) should support his family. The new, more modest, goal has a worker paid one-half of what it takes to support a family of four.

To meet this goal will require further increases in productivity, most of which will come from automation, which further depresses employment rates. More workers will be better paid, yet more people will be out of work, unless there is a corresponding rise in labor-intensive, local jobs in agriculture and boutique, handicraft industries, or a shorter work week.

Finally, more companies are likely to follow entrepreneur Jack Stack's advice to offer equity to a broad base of employees to increase their engagement with their jobs.

Customers: As everything becomes more expensive, customers will become choosier and buy less. They will increasingly demand to know whether products qualify as healthy and humane. And broad, innovative applications of those 400-plus social and environmental indexes will help customers choose products made by companies that pay fairly and work to tangibly reduce their environmental damage.

Communities: As travel and shipping become more expensive over the next fifty years, we are likely to see at least the partial restoration of a company's sense of locality. This can help make local communities stronger and more resilient, and more active in the effort to attract and keep beneficial employers.

Responsible businesses will have to work more closely with NGOs and interest groups to reduce environmental harm and improve working conditions throughout the supply chain. Trade associations and third-party verification organizations will become more important as more companies benchmark their social and environmental standards, work to raise the bar, and have their efforts to meet them monitored and verified by independent parties. Above all, companies will have to work as true partners with their suppliers, in a climate of trust. Profit will come not from taking advantage of one another, but from efficiencies gained by understanding each other's problems and meeting each other's needs.

Nature: As customers learn more about the consequences of ravaging the natural world at our current pace, they will pressure companies to do far more, more quickly, to reduce the damage they cause. Rising cost will constitute its own pressure on companies to adopt more responsible practices. Expenses will rise for natural resources (especially energy and water) and for waste disposal. Companies, not individuals, generate 75 percent of the trash that reaches the landfill or incinerator. Packaging, for which the producer is responsible, is disposed of almost instantly by the consumer and comprises a third of all waste.

The need to use less energy and generate less waste will in turn require companies to conduct life-cycle analyses (LCA) of their products. The LCA teaches a company how to reduce the environmental impact of its products from their origins as raw materials (derived from water, the soil, or underground) through their manufacture, useful life, and eventual disposal. Finally, companies will have to track environmental performance through all business reporting systems.

It is essential to decouple the definition of economic health from economic growth in the use of materials and energy. It is not pie in the sky to say so. Germany, Japan, and China, among other governments, have announced their intention to create "circular economies" that promote reduction, reuse, and recycling of materials. Japan passed a law in 2000 to increase resource productivity by 60 percent, increase recycling by 40 to 50 percent, and reduce waste disposal by 60 percent by 2010. As of 2008, it was on track, according to World Watch's 2011 report.

The U.S. needs to follow suit and create its own circular economy. This would require eliminating government subsidies and tax breaks for industrial agriculture, oil and gas production, and other nonrenewable resources, so that prices would reflect true costs. The U.S. Treasury, for example, pays $2 billion a year to support the price of chemically intensive conventional cotton grown in California and Texas.

In a post-consumerist society, it's critical that we stop using the gross domestic product (GDP) as a barometer of social health. As economist Joseph Stiglitz puts it, we need to expand the idea of GDP to include noneconomic factors. In October 2010, the U.K., following the lead of Bhutan, Canada, and France, adopted (with some nervousness on the part of its Conservative government) a "happiness index" that defines quality of life more broadly than does GDP. The U.K. index includes metrics on job satisfaction and economic security, satisfying relations with friends and relatives, having a say on local and national issues, health, education, environmental health, personal security, and volunteer activities.

Were we to grow less distracted by our consumerism and consumption, and to spend more time with friends and family, or work with people we want to help, or learn something we have always wanted to be able to do, wouldn't that make up for missing yet another sale at the mall? The pursuit of national wealth through trade of increasingly useless things has for a few decades kept us in more clothes than we need, but has nothing to do with the pursuit of happiness. And it simply no longer works.

{ 34 }

It is financially unsustainable for the world economy to require 3 percent annual growth, which corresponds to the 3 percent growth a company must now maintain to outpace inflation and prevent job loss. Yet the economy in advanced societies no longer creates sufficient well-paid jobs; the speed of automation outpaces that of job creation. All rich countries face high levels of debt because fewer well-paid workers pay the taxes to sustain outlays for health care, education, and the military.

Can a company do many things right and be *irresponsible?* Imagine a business that returns a tidy profit, treats its employees well, makes the best-quality product possible, gives generously to the community, rebuilds its headquarters to LEED standards and throws in a rooftop garden—but makes land mines. Not in the U.S., where it has been illegal to make land mines since 1997, but offshore, through its supply chain.

Land mines hurt mostly civilians: 158 countries (the U.S. not included) have called for an international ban.

Many companies, some of them highly admired in the pages of business journals and on Wall Street, do make, in this country, things like cigarettes, the extra-large version of the Cadillac Escalade, Lucky Charms, hollow-point bullets, baby toys containing endocrine-disrupting phthalates, and lead-containing lipstick. Companies that behave responsibly in some important way may also hire teams of lobbyists to discredit worthy but unfavorable science, or export to developing countries harmful or dirty products banned in the U.S., Europe, and Japan. It isn't enough for companies to argue that they're simply meeting customer demand: to make a bad product is to do bad business.

In the coming decades, as customers become more insistent, environmental laws become more restrictive, resources become less plentiful and more costly, and investors more demanding, every company will face competitors who embrace all the elements of business responsibility—not always because it's the right thing to do, but because it is essential to being successful. To compete, a company will have to be at least as responsible as its competitors.

More than thirty-five years ago, the authors of this book had lunch together at Myrt's Cottage Café, a greasy spoon a block away run by beehived waitresses who had for decades dished out biscuits and gravy and grilled cheese sandwiches to workers in the oil fields up the street: Johnny Cash may have had coffee and a smoke at Myrt's at some point during the mid-fifties, when he played the honkytonk across the street.

At the time of our workingman's lunch, Yvon was paying himself $800 a month, and Vincent, because he didn't surf and hung around to answer the phones, had recently been promoted to sales manager, with a raise to $3 an hour. The two of us talked about doing what people were telling us we had to do to become more of a real business—hire reps, get out a new catalog, exhibit at a trade show, maybe take out a couple of ads.

At one point Yvon turned to Vincent and said, "If I did everything right, did everything the experts say I *have* to do to succeed in business, I'd go broke."

We also remember a legend an old garmento told us around the same time about how to make money in clothing: Remove the paper pattern, called the marker, that lies on top of a fabric stack to guide the cutter, crumple or "shrink" the marker, place it back on the fabric, then run the blade. That half of one percent of fabric you save becomes your profit.

Those stories come back to us now as we discuss what a responsible company does or doesn't do. The term itself is necessary shorthand; there is no responsible company, only responsible companies of varying degrees, who act strategically to do less harm while improving, not sacrificing, the health of the business.

Can we boil this down?

Science journalist Daniel Goleman in *Ecological Intelligence* offered three simple, yet remarkably comprehensive rules for reducing environmental harm: "Know your impacts, favor improvement, share what you learn." This applies to us all, in large and small companies, as we begin or continue to act.

CHAPTER 4
MEANINGFUL WORK

E VERYONE WANTS meaningful work, but what exactly makes work meaningful? And what does meaningful work have to do with the responsible company?

At its heart, to have meaningful work is to do something you love to do and are good at doing for a living. Most people don't know, at first, what they love best. What they become best at develops by trial and error or by accident. We're all good at something: with words or numbers, or we work with our hands, or we work best outside.

One of the authors of this book, Yvon, would rather spend his day picking apricots or hoeing his garden than sit at as desk and stare into a computer screen. Repetitive, rhythmic work need not be numbing, as anyone who has spent all day hammering pitons at the forge knows: it can be enlightening. Or joyous, as in the scene in Anna Karenina where the aristocrat Levin scythes wheat with his peasants: he can't keep up with them until he learns how to fall into the rhythm. The other author, Vincent, who once spent a muddy October picking grapes for his living, would rather spend his day at the keyboard than tending his garden.

Meaningful work is doing things you love to do, often, though not always, with other people. No responsible company can function well without a lot of different people doing things they love to do in concert with others. Doing what you love to do makes work meaningful. Doing the right thing, with others, makes work meaningful.

Although this book is not a history of Patagonia, this chapter draws on our experience to show how one company's responsible actions (some small, some large) helped make work meaningful for its employees, and how responsible behavior, as it becomes cumulative, also makes a company smarter, more nimble, and potentially more successful.

{ 38 }

In its early days, Patagonia attracted the disaffected—people who loved climbing and surfing or vagabonding best, and would come back to Ventura to pick up work for a few months at a time. Or people who had a degree in physics or biology, who for one reason or another, usually the inability or unwillingness to fit into an academic culture, changed course. They would find a home at Patagonia because they found the culture congenially filled with other outsiders (the way Paris or Manhattan was at times for twentieth-century artists). A guidance counselor at Santa Paula High School told Kristine Tompkins's mother not to waste her money sending her daughter to college. Kristine, the unmotivated and indifferent student, would at age thirty become Patagonia's fast-learning CEO during its critical early days (and in midlife would, with her husband Doug Tompkins, help save or restore over two million acres of exhausted ranchland and surrounding wilderness in Chile and Argentina).

We did not bristle with overachievers who could find reward in what we saw as the real world. Instead, we attracted bright, restless, unconventional people like Kris who hadn't felt the call toward a vocation, and others who had sought and then abandoned one, or had pursued one that couldn't provide a living.

Many Patagonia employees turned out to have a vocation working for a small, quirky company where no one knew what they couldn't do, so ended up doing things they had no idea they could do, in the company of others doing the same thing. Doing something as silly as working in the clothing business turned out to engage the intelligence, imagination, and social needs of our unconventional, anti-establishment employees.

Today, Patagonia does employ a lot of people who found their vocation early and answered it. They were drawn to color from infancy, or started sewing clothes of their own design when they were ten, {39} or earned a graduate degree in textile chemistry, or always drew and went to art school. We have, more than we care to admit, several MBAs working in the company, some of whom really love business for itself, others who earned the degree to help them do well in life. (We're not awash in entrepreneurs, who by definition would rather be working for themselves.)

Patagonia also has bright locals who grew up in the area, feel at home here, don't want to leave, and find our company the most interesting place in town to work. It's the best place in town for women to work. Conversely, we have some top executives who don't want to live in Ventura because they don't like it or their families are settled elsewhere; they can afford to commute and do.

And a number of people work for Patagonia, and seek to come to Patagonia, because they think the company's values coincide with their own. That deep sympathy provides the extra motivation it takes to stay levelheaded and alert when a workday gets difficult. It keeps people engaged when they have to figure out a new fabric source because the old one is found to have a toxic dye; or when they have to negotiate with a factory to invest in ventilation because someone from our sourcing department has smelled something disturbing during a visit; or when they must work with a vendor to increase the recycled content of catalog paper without reducing the quality of the printing or raising the price. Doing the right thing motivates us to work past the point where we might otherwise give up.

Meaningful work, it turns out, is doing not only what we love but also giving back to the world. The two combined create the ground for a kind of ordinary human excellence that any business can treasure.

Every company has to encourage and cultivate this ordinary human excellence if it is to become more nimble, responsive, and responsible. Every time people in the company do something new that was formerly thought impossible, they contribute significantly to the company's culture, and to the sense that much will be possible in the future. We can think of several critical moments in Patagonia's past that changed our sense of the possible, moments in which we became a more responsible, and thus more motivated, company without necessarily knowing we were doing so (we were just trying to sell some clothes for a living!). The moments turned out to be cumulative. It isn't our intention to write a new version of Patagonia's early history, but we'd like to recount some of the moments that increased our sense of responsibility, and our capacity to act responsibly; we'd like to show how these moments built on one another. The intention here is not to celebrate our own experience but to tell some stories that you might find reassuring and instructive, and helpful in the course of your own work.

Climbing Clean

In 1972, Chouinard Equipment was still a small company (about

$400,000 a year in sales), but it had become the largest supplier of climbing hardware in the U.S. With the increased popularity of climbing, and its concentration on the same well-tried routes (in Yosemite Valley, El Dorado Canyon, the Shawangunks, etc.), our reusable hard-steel pitons had become environmental villains. The same fragile cracks had to endure repeated hammering of pitons during both placement and removal, and the disfiguring was severe. After an ascent of the degraded Nose route on El Capitan, which had been pristine a few summers earlier, Yvon and partner Tom Frost decided to phase out of the piton business. It was a huge risk: pitons were the mainstay of the business. But the change had to be made for reasons both moral and practical: the routes were beautiful and satisfying and shouldn't be ruined; and to ruin them would put an end to, or greatly reduce, the possibilities for climbing in the most popular areas, and thus eventually hurt our business.

There was an alternative: aluminum chocks that could be wedged in and removed by hand without the use of a hammer. Hexentrics and stoppers made their first appearance in the Chouinard Equipment catalog in 1972.

That catalog opened with an editorial from the owners on the environmental hazards of pitons. A fourteen-page essay by Sierra climber Doug Robinson on how to use chocks began with a powerful paragraph:

> There is a word for it, and the word is clean. Climbing with only nuts and runners for protection is clean climbing. Clean because the rock is left unaltered by the passing climber. Clean because nothing is hammered into the rock and then hammered back out, leaving the rock scarred and the next climber's experience less natural. Clean because the climber's protection leaves little trace of his ascension. Clean is climbing the rock without changing it; a step closer to organic climbing for the natural man.

Within a few months of the catalog's mailing, the piton business had atrophied; chocks sold faster than they could be made. In the tin sheds of Chouinard Equipment, the steady pounding rhythm of the drop hammer gave way to the high-pitched whine of the multiple-drill jig.

At Chouinard Equipment, we learned that we could inspire our customers to do less harm simply by making them aware of the problem and offering a solution. We also learned that by addressing the problem we had forced ourselves to make a better product: chocks were lighter than pitons and as or more secure. We might not have risked the obsolescence of our piton business just to sell something new. But doing the right thing motivated us—and turned out to be good business.

{42} **Befriending the Ventura River**

If you took a train from France to Italy around the time Chouinard Equipment started making chocks, you might have noticed the Italians in your compartment tossing their lunch wrappers, crumpled cigarette packs, and wine bottles cheerfully out the window into the country-side, until the train crossed the border into Italy, at which time the same people would turn fastidious and collect their garbage to toss in the waste bin. One did not trash the mother country.

At Chouinard Equipment, we were the opposite. We cared much about the mountains but not much about Ventura, a funky little oil patch and lemon-packing town with a lot of junk shops, hazardous waste, and a dead river. Nature was something you drove to.

In our travels, we saw what was happening in the remote corners of the world: creeping pollution and deforestation, the slow, then not so slow, disappearance of fish and wildlife. And we saw what was happening closer to home: thousand-year-old sequoias succumbing to L.A. smog, the thinning of life in tide pools and kelp beds, the rampant development of the land along the coast. But we did not see what was happening at home.

We began to read about global warming, the cutting and burning of tropical forests, the rapid loss of groundwater and topsoil, acid rain, the ruin of rivers and creeks from silting-over dams—descriptions of environmental destruction reinforced by what we saw with our own eyes and smelled with our own noses on our journeys. And we slowly became aware that uphill environmental battles fought by small, dedicated groups of people to save patches of land and stretches of water could yield significant results.

Around that time, a group of us went to a city council meeting to help protect a local surf break. We knew vaguely that the Ventura River had once been a major steelhead salmon habitat. During the forties, two dams had been built, and water diverted. Except for winter rains, the only water left at the river mouth flowed from the sewage plant. {43} At the city council meeting, several experts testified that the river was dead and that channeling the mouth would have no effect on remaining bird- and wildlife, or on our surf break.

Then Mark Capelli, a shy-looking 25-year-old biology student, gave a slide show of photos he had taken along the river—of the birds that lived in the willows, of the muskrats and water snakes, of eels that spawned in the estuary. When he showed a slide of a steelhead smolt, everyone stood up to cheer. Yes, fifty or so steelhead still came to spawn in our "dead" river.

The development plan was defeated. Patagonia gave Mark office space and a mailbox, and small contributions to help him fight the river's battle. As more development plans cropped up, the Friends of the Ventura River worked to defeat them, and to clean up the water and increase its flow. Wildlife increased, and a few more steelhead began to spawn.

Mark taught us three important lessons: that a grassroots effort could make a difference; that a degraded habitat could, with effort, be restored; and that the natural world wasn't just in the faraway silent places. Nature still lived outside wilderness, lived where we lived, in our funky oil and ag town, and we could help give it some space to thrive. We had a responsibility to do so.

Kids

During the early seventies, one of the co-owners of Chouinard Equipment, Dorene Frost, used to bring her daughter Marna to work; no one minded. After the Chouinards' son Fletcher was born, Malinda brought him in; then other workers, as they had babies, brought them in as well. And so on. By the early eighties, you could find baby blankets draped over computer monitors, and rattles and toy trains littered the floor. And of course kids cried.

The noise prompted a discussion about providing day care, not as a progressive measure—childcare in the workplace in those days was so rare we didn't even know it was progressive. The mothers who worked for us simply wanted to be near their babies, to breastfeed or comfort them when needed.

The men at the company, including the co-authors, and the women without kids, including the CEO, didn't agree that Patagonia should devote its scarce cash or space to running a "nursery school." But, backed by the moms, Malinda doggedly pursued her cause and eventually won out. The kids stayed, and they have made a difference to the quality of our workday.

First, the sight and sound of children playing in their yard makes the place feel more human and less corporate. Second, the presence of children makes adults conscious of their responsibilities as mammals: grownups, first; employees, second. Third, our childcare, maternal and paternal leave, and flextime policies allow women to advance in the company. Moreover, Anita Furtaw, who has run the childcare center for two decades, knows a lot about raising children; new parents have been grateful for her advice and the quality of the care she and her staff provide. The kids grow up well; we're as proud of that as we are of the clothes we produce.

Providing on-site childcare turned out to be a good business decision. Being one of the first companies in California to have on-site childcare made it easier for us to risk doing things other companies hadn't done or had done rarely, like provide flex-time or job sharing. We have a very low employee turnover rate, especially among parents of school-age children. The presence of kids and the introduction of childcare taught us that if there is some quality about the workplace you love and don't want to lose, don't. It costs Patagonia roughly $50,000, on average, to recruit, train, and get up to speed a new employee; if we want to make any money, it's a good idea to keep the ones we have happy and fully engaged.

Environmental Giving

Once Mark Capelli taught us what could be done for a degraded local landscape, we knew that beloved patches of land and stretches of water all over the country could be saved or restored; lots of small groups, with much passion and no money, had begun to work on behalf of the places they loved.

If a mailbox and a bit of cash could make a difference for Mark, so could small grants for others trying to save or restore habitat. Patagonia began to make regular donations of $1,000 here and $5,000 there. We favored the little groups no other corporation would touch, rather than NGOs with big staffs, high overheads, and corporate connections.

In 1986, the company committed to annually donate 10 percent of profits to these groups. We did so for two reasons. First, we wanted to help. Second, we believed we owed the earth a tax for the industrial impact of our business activities. We consider our giving a cost of doing business, not charity. We later upped the ante to an annual one percent of sales, or 10 percent of profits, whichever is greater: what we do affects the planet whether or not we make a profit.

In addition, every two years Patagonia hosts a "Tools for Grassroots Activists" conference to teach marketing, publicity, and lobbying skills to seventy-five selected participants from the groups with whom we work. The speakers are first-rate. We are always moved by the dedication and intelligence of the activists.

At Patagonia, environmental grant-giving is by now deeply embedded in the culture. Employees elected to serve on Patagonia's Grants Council direct the giving each year. They choose the groups and determine the size of each grant. We also run an environmental internship program. Employees apply to work full-time for one of our grantees on a project of their choosing for up to six weeks.

In 2002, Yvon and Craig Mathews, the owner of Blue Ribbon {46} Flies, a venerable Yellowstone angler's shop, created 1% for the Planet, an alliance of companies that pledge one percent or more of their annual sales to environmental causes. 1% for the Planet now has nearly 1,500 members (mostly small businesses, in more than forty countries), which annually donate to more than 2,500 nonprofits.

Joining 1% has been a good business decision for its members. During the depths of the 2008-09 recession we talked with the other four of the five largest companies who participate in 1% and each of us reported record sales. In a downturn, people do business with fewer companies; when they spend less, they do it with companies they respect and trust more.

Patagonia also undertook in its catalogs and, later, on our website, environmental education campaigns of one to three years in duration, to raise the awareness of our customers about an environmental topic that had not yet received much general attention. One year, we advocated a more sensible, less car-centric, master plan for Yosemite National Park. We have campaigned on behalf of the survival of wild salmon and against the introduction of genetically modified foods. We campaigned against NAFTA because it lowered labor and environmental standards. We have worked to remove outdated dams that keep fish from reaching their spawning ground. We have alerted people to the deteriorating condition of the oceans; the need for wildlife corridors so wild mammals can migrate through fragmented habitat in a time of climate change; and how little freshwater there is left on this planet, as aquifers dry up and rivers cease to reach the sea.

Getting Our House in Order

Only after we gained the confidence to assail some of the enemies of nature did we become capable of recognizing the foe we had long overlooked in the mirror. We still had only a partial view of the enemy that was us. By the late 1980s, we could acknowledge that our company of several hundred people engaged directly in activities that polluted {47} the earth or wasted resources: we flew on planes, printed great runs of catalogs from felled trees, drastically remodeled buildings to house our stores. We did not recognize, however, the harm we did as a maker of clothes. We were dependent on our supply chain, we thought, and not in a position to get them to change their ways.

Although we had never been shy about asking our fabric suppliers to make changes that would improve our clothing's performance, we had not yet learned to ask them to use recycled materials or investigate the wastewater policies of the dye houses that worked with the mills, or check too closely into working conditions on the sewing-factory floor.

Instead, we began to change what we controlled directly, such as the production of our catalogs (we helped make a quality stock with high post-consumer-recycled content commercially viable for the paper mills) or the build-out of new and remodeling of old retail store locations, using VOC-free paints, recycled wood and wallboard, and energy-efficient lighting. In 1996, our new distribution center in Reno achieved a 60 percent reduction in energy use through solar-tracking skylights and radiant heating; recycled content was used there for everything from rebar to carpet to urinal partitions. The following year, when we built a three-story office building in Ventura on the former site of Myrt's Cottage Café, we used 95 percent recycled materials. By 2006, we had the accumulated experience and confidence to success-fully seek LEED certification for the expansion of our Reno distribution center, even though building to this standard was a first for both our contractor and the Reno area.

Poisoning Our People

By 1988, we had taken several steps to get our house in order, but we had not yet changed the way we made clothing.

Within days after the opening of our Boston store, its staff began to experience headaches during their shifts. We had the air tested: we learned that the ventilation system was faulty and off-gassing form-aldehyde was poisoning our staff. A typical business response might have been to fix the ventilation system to make the headaches go away. At the time, all we knew about formaldehyde we remembered from biology class: the chemical in the jar with the sheep's heart. But the source of formaldehyde in the store turned out to be the finish on our cotton clothes, added by the mill to prevent shrinkage and wrinkling.

It dawned on us that we really didn't know how to make clothing responsibly, and we were failing as a business to lead an examined life. What other harms were we causing?

We researched formaldehyde and discovered that it could cause cancer of the nose, nasal cavity, and throat. (The Environmental Protec-tion Agency [EPA] would acknowledge these dangers two decades later when Hurricane Katrina victims got sick from the formaldehyde in their FEMA trailers.) To minimize the use of formaldehyde yet avoid increased shrinkage or wrinkling, we used higher-quality, long-staple cotton, altered the way the fiber was spun, and pre-shrank the fabric. Although this added some cost, it was important to us not to sacrifice quality in the course of reducing environmental harm. None of us wanted to have to iron our pants or send them to the dry cleaner to be treated with more chemicals.

We had been conducting our business like any other clothing company. We'd chosen cotton fabrics on the basis of their texture and durability and sent the sample off to a cut-and-sew factory, which would source from a mill, which sourced from a broker, which bundled its raw-cotton purchases, depending on the spot price, from multiple countries. We had no idea where the cotton came from, let alone how it was finished.

So in 1991, we commissioned a study to assess the environmental impacts of the four fibers most commonly used in our clothes: cotton, {49} polyester, nylon, and wool. We had no idea how badly cotton, our most commonly used natural fiber, would fare. It turned out to be not much more natural than nylon.

It's a horrific story. To prepare soil for planting cotton, workers spray organophosphates (which can damage the human central nervous system) to kill off all other living organisms. The soil, once treated, is doornail dead (five pesticide-free years have to pass before earthworms, an indication of soil health, can return). Such soil requires intensive use of artificial fertilizers to hold the cotton plants in place. Rainwater runoff from cotton fields contributes significantly to the growth of ocean dead zones. Cotton fields, representing 2.5 percent of cultivated land, ingest 15 percent of chemical insecticides used in agriculture and 10 percent of pesticides. About one-tenth of 1 percent of these chemicals reach the pests they target.

Genetically modified Bt (*Bacillus thuringiensis*) cotton, introduced in the past decade, reduces pesticide use initially by more specifically targeting leaf-eating bollworms. China, which planted Bt cotton on a large scale in the early 2000s, found that after a few seasons, grass bugs and other pests immune to Bt stepped into the breach left by the bollworms; wholesale spraying had to be resumed.

Cotton fields contribute 165 million metric tons of greenhouse gas emissions every year. A conventional cotton field stinks; its chemicals burn the eyes and nauseate the stomach. Before harvesting in non-frost regions like California, cotton has to be sprayed by a cropduster with the defoliant Paraquat, about half of which hits its target. The rest settles over the neighbors' fields and into our streams.

None of this is necessary. No cotton was grown this way before World War II, when many of the chemicals now used in agriculture were first developed as nerve gases for warfare.

When we first started looking for alternatives, organic cotton was available from a few family farmers in California and Texas. We experimented. At first we made only T-shirts with organic cotton. Then, after several trips to the San Joaquin Valley, where we could smell the selenium ponds and see the lunar landscape of cotton fields, we asked a critical question: How could we continue to make products that laid waste to the earth this way? In the fall of 1994, we made the decision to take our cotton sportswear 100 percent organic by 1996.

We had eighteen months to make the switch for sixty-six products, and less than a year to line up the fabric. There simply wasn't enough organic cotton commercially available to buy through brokers, so we had to go directly to the few farmers who had gone back to organic methods. We had to talk to the certifiers so that all the fiber could be traced back to the bale. And then we had to go to the ginners and spinners and persuade them to clean their equipment before and after running what for them would be very low quantities. The spinners in particular objected to organic cotton because it was full of leaves and stems and sticky from aphids. Our most creative partner, in Thailand, solved the problem by freezing the cotton before spinning.

Due to the resourcefulness and open-minded of our new partners, we succeeded. Every Patagonia garment made of cotton in 1996 was organic and has been ever since. Our cotton odyssey taught us our responsibility for what happens in Patagonia's name at every step in the supply chain.

That first fabric assessment also taught us that oil-based polyester could be made less harmful by using recycled sources rather than oil fresh out of the well. We learned how to make a fleece jacket from twenty-five quart-size plastic soda bottles, melted down and extruded into fiber. We learned later that the most efficient way to make polyester fiber was from polyester clothing at the end of its useful life, melted down, and extruded anew.

We've learned since what textiles do to water. You can now see, {51} on Google Earth satellite images, the pollution of the Pearl River where it flows indigo into the South China Sea. Indigo is the color of the discharge from the world's major jeans factories upstream in Xingtang.

The textile industry is one of the most chemically intensive industries on earth, second only to agriculture, and the world's largest polluter of increasingly scarce freshwater. The World Bank estimates nearly 20 percent of industrial water pollution comes from textile dyeing and treatment. They've also identified seventy-two toxic chemicals in our water that have textile dyes as their source; these dyes, when not controlled in the workplace, can compromise the health of employees. The textile industry is also a water hog, for coal- or wood-powered steam to fuel mills and for water-intensive dyeing and finishing processes.

Wastewater that goes—often illegally—untreated or partially treated returns to a river, where it heats the water, increases its pH, and saturates it with dyes, finishes, and fixatives, which in turn leave a residue of salts and metals that leech into farmland or settle into the viscera of fish. In 2010, both China and India closed textile mills on a vast scale for violation of pollution laws. In Madras, the government required the local power company to discontinue service to 700 mills until they complied with the law.

We know that the water it takes to irrigate a single Patagonia polo shirt could provide a day's drinking water for 900 people; and that fifteen years from now, between one-third and one-half of the world's population will live in an area famished by drought.

The freshwater crisis has been apparent for more than a decade. Yet only recently have we specified that all fabric used in Patagonia products be dyed in plants that thoroughly treat their wastewater before returning it to a river. Michel Morger and Thomas Schrieder, two industry veterans who wanted to create a cutting-edge dyeing and finishing facility, fulfill this mission in the industrial heart of the Los Angeles basin. Their company, Swisstex California, can handle large orders or small and turn them around quickly. Computerized controls keep water usage to a minimum, just enough to run the pumps. Swisstex uses half as much water as an average dyehouse in the U.S. A state-of-the-art wastewater heat recovery system enables it to use wastewater energy to preheat incoming cold water and water is recycled as many times as possible. Their laboratory is robotized and the dye machines automated to reduce downtime and the potential for error. The idea is to produce high-quality results the first time: about 10 percent of fabric has to be scrapped industrywide because of poor dyeing; 10 to 20 percent has to be re-dyed to meet specifications. As all of us in business know, returns for poor quality and rework are sinkholes for profit. It does not cost us more to use Swisstex.

The Footprint Chronicles

By 2005, Patagonia had not yet created a corporate social responsibility report (CSR), which most mid- and large-sized (usually publicly traded) companies already issued. NGOs, advocacy groups and journalists had become accustomed to the CSR as a tool for examining the comparative business practices of corporations. We drafted an initial report in the vague, cream-of-wheat monotone characteristic of environmental- and social-responsibility reporting. Such reports tell you how much the company gave to the symphony but not how many square miles it destroyed in the Niger Delta.

We wanted to come up with a more transparent and compelling way to report on our activity—or lack of it; we wanted to engage our customers as well as those numbed by CSR rhetoric. So we developed the Footprint Chronicles, a mildly interactive mini-website that, in its first season, traced five Patagonia products geographically from design, to fiber (at its point of origin), to weaving or knitting, to dyeing, to sewing, to delivery at our Reno warehouse. For each of the five products we also calculated carbon emissions, energy use, and waste, as well as the distance traveled from origin to warehouse. We posted this information on the product's online selling page as well as on the Chronicles' website.

It is important to note that Patagonia's dedicated environmental staff for products numbered all of two. The small size of the department was deliberate: we wanted the reduction of environmental harm to be part of everyone's job. We did not want to create a separate bureaucracy that might clash unproductively with our product-quality or sourcing staff, or give that staff a reason to make environmental considerations secondary because someone else would handle them in their stead. We wanted our enviros to be a welcome, well-regarded resource throughout the company.

One drawback to our decision to keep the department small was that we did not have the capacity to do a complete life-cycle analysis (LCA) for a great number of products. To date, we have been able to calculate, and post online, limited LCAs for about 150 products, or

{ 53 }

about 20 percent of our product line, which represents about 80 percent of sales. In the future, we plan to adopt, when they are complete, the independent methodology established by the Outdoor Industry Association's Eco Index and the Sustainable Apparel Coalition's version of it. It is our hope that within five years any customer who owns a smart phone will be able to scan the QR code on any Patagonia product to learn its social and environmental impact.

The idea behind the Footprint Chronicles was to examine Patagonia's full life and habits as a company. We wanted to look beyond our employees to every person who worked on Patagonia products on farms, and in mills, dye houses, and factories. We had about 500 people on our payroll engaged in design, testing, sales, marketing, and distribution, whereas up to 10,000 people at any given time worked on Patagonia products throughout the supply chain. We wanted to teach ourselves { 54 } more deeply about our own business. It was time to bring to the surface the unintended harmful consequences of making all Patagonia clothes. Harm done on an industrial scale could be reduced on an industrial scale.

Maxport, a factory near Hanoi, made some of our most sophisticated technical outerwear, paid its workers well, and maintained a factory that could only be called beautiful. "Your customers," said owner Jef Stokes, "have a right to know if their jacket was sewn by a 12-year-old girl working all day for a bowl of rice." The customer had a right to know, indeed, if people who made Patagonia clothes were paid legally, treated fairly, and worked in decent conditions. The customer had a right to know whether the indigo dyes in his jeans ended up in the Pearl River, whether the cotton was organic or chemical-intensive, or whether the water used came from rainfall or from an irrigation ditch that relied on a dam.

We are no longer, as in the days of Chouinard Equipment, a pre-Industrial Revolution workshop built around a courtyard, a kind of village business. Most of the people who do most of the work to assemble our clothes are poor, darker skinned, and female. They punch a time clock and work at a machine in a long row marked by a number hung from a ceiling. Day after day, they sew clothes for Patagonia, and on days they don't sew for us, they sew for our competitors. What we're willing to pay their employer helps determine their wages.

What does Patagonia owe these workers?

From farm to mill to factory, wages are low, as they have been since the beginning of the Industrial Revolution. For two centuries textile mills and sewing factories have provided entry-level jobs for people in transition from an agricultural subsistence to an industrial economy. Once wages in a region rise, people find better jobs. The factories pick up and move on to a new, rural region or country where a fresh crop of people can be enticed to leave farms for the promise of regular pay.

When we got into the apparel business forty years ago, high-quality sportswear production had already moved from the United States to Hong Kong, then still a British colony. Over time, the epicenter for sportswear drifted from Hong Kong to the mainland, then to north and inland in China, then finally to Vietnam and Thailand. When sewing factories first arrived in a rural area, the managers would recruit young women from the region's farms and set them up in barracks. The women would work hard for a few years to earn their dowry, then go home. Meanwhile, a town would grow up around the factory, and the barracks would no longer be needed.

This idea for unified housing and labor originated in the 1830s in the United States. When the first big integrated textile mills were established in Lowell and Lawrence, Massachusetts, local farmers considered factory work beneath them but agreed to send their daughters to the mills. The girls and women had one-year contracts and lived together in boardinghouses, six to a room, twenty-five to a house.

On a visit from England, Charles Dickens praised the mills' working and living conditions, noting pianos in the boardinghouse parlors and a literary magazine written, as the cover boasted, by "factory operatives." By today's standards, though, conditions were cruel: women worked from seven to seven; windows were shut to ensure high humidity to keep the yarn moist; cotton lint floated through the air and into the lungs; and an extraordinary level of noise sounded from the mill's crudely calibrated looms.

Once the New England towns grew up around their mills, the boardinghouses closed. By the end of the nineteenth century, the factory labor base had shifted from farm girls to immigrant families. Our own family took part in this history: they sold their farm in Québec to emigrate south to work the looms of the cotton and woolen mills along the Androscoggin River. The system was efficient. In 1908, in the company of his parents and ten siblings, Yvon's nine-year old father took the train to Lewiston, Maine. The Grand Trunk Railroad Depot stood opposite the Bates Manufacturing Company's hiring hall. Behind the hall lay a sprawl of four-decker wooden tenements known as P'tit Canada. A family could arrive at the station, secure jobs for everyone who could physically work (age six on up), then walk half a block to rent their rooms. The French Canadians took work that all Yankees by then, including girls and women, regarded as beneath them.

Was it meaningful work? Such a term wouldn't have occurred to our immigrant relatives. They were of that generation in transition from meaningful but hardscrabble life bound to the land, to an industrial life of low-paid work for long hours in uncomfortable, if not unsafe, conditions. They were no longer peasants; they had become essentially industrial soldiers with no independent control over most of their waking hours. Their new life met their basic needs for food and shelter, as well as their social needs: their friends worked alongside them. According to the view of psychologist Abraham Maslow, however, our family members had yet to meet the two highest, most complex requirements in the hierarchy of needs: a sense of worth and self-fulfillment. It was Maslow's view that needs must be met in the order of their importance for survival: basics first, self-fulfillment last. We suspect that as our family members advanced their basic needs, they lost hefty measures of self-worth and self-fulfillment. When they left the farm for the mill, they gained a regular income, which made life easier, but as overworked laborers in a deafening work space, they lost their autonomy, sense of purpose, and their connection to nature. Farm life had been harsh, and in bad years dangerous, but not demeaning in this new way.

The mills eventually moved south from New England to the Carolinas, in successful pursuit of cheaper, nonunion labor. Today, the garment industry has moved offshore to Asia and South America. The marathon chase for cheaper labor, sped up by thirty years of globalization, will within a decade or so play itself out in Africa, the last place a factory can go to pay people too little. But half of that continent's billion inhabitants already own cell phones. In the post-consumerist society, even mill workers and sewing operators will make a living wage. They will also have the right to have their highest needs met: the need to be treated respectfully; the need to give the best of themselves; and the need to feel that what they are doing helps, not harms society. No work, anywhere, should be meaningless.

Patagonia doesn't own farms, mills, or factories. Most of our employees have never been any place where Patagonia clothes are produced at any stage. Yet what is done in our name must not remain invisible to us. We are responsible for all the workers who make our goods and for all that goes into a piece of clothing that bears a Patagonia label.

It took us a long time to ask ourselves what we owe people who work for others in our supply chain. We had high sewing standards, even for casual sportswear, and exacting standards for technical clothes. To meet quality requirements, our production staff had always been drawn to clean, well-lighted factories that employed experienced sewing operators. Although we had always bargained with our factories over price and terms, we never chased lowest-cost labor.

Yet when a labor-rights group revealed that Kathie Lee Gifford's clothing line for Wal-Mart was sewn by 12-year-olds, we wondered whether we were doing anything close. When Kathie Lee Gifford said she had no idea, we believed her. We knew how little we knew about our own supply chain. What measures did our factories take to prevent or deal with a fire? Did they use needle guards to prevent injuries? How many hours a week did the women sew? We didn't know. Even in good factories, employees can be forced to work long hours, especially when a company like ours re-orders a hot-selling item and pressures for early delivery.

In 1999, we accepted an invitation to join a task force created by President Clinton (in response to the Gifford scandal) to end child labor and improve garment-factory conditions worldwide. Out of this task force came the Fair Labor Association (FLA), an independent nonprofit monitoring organization dedicated to fair pay and decent working conditions. FLA's Workplace Code of Conduct prohibits child labor, forced labor, violence, sexual and psychological harassment, and racial discrimination. It guarantees minimum legal or prevailing wage, whichever is higher, overtime wages (with limits on the number overtime hours allowed, a sticky issue), healthy and safe working conditions, and freedom of association to join a union (though independent unions are outlawed in China and Vietnam). Patagonia has its own Code of Conduct that prevents factories from subcontracting work without our permission and requires them to maintain a quality-improvement plan.

Before placing an initial order with a factory, Patagonia has a member of its social/environmental responsibility team visit to verify conditions. This team member can break the deal. Our quality director has similar veto power over the sourcing department's decision to take on a new factory.

During the early 2000s, we made the poor choice to expand our factory base in search of lower-cost labor. At one point we dealt with more than 100 factories, more than we could handle; we no longer knew many of the people with whom we were dealing or what conditions were like on the factory floor. The result: poor product quality, late delivery, expensive rework, long inspection times at our Reno warehouse, customer dissatisfaction, and loss of profit incurred by honoring customer returns.

We then reduced our factory count by a third and bolstered our relationships with the people with whom we continued to do business; their factories continuously improved quality, including the quality of life on the job for their workers. We now work with some factories we admire and with whom we feel a strong kinship. Everyone from the sewing operator to the factory chief cares about the quality of their work and their day. These factories, which include Maxport, pay better than prevailing wage, provide a healthy subsidized lunch and low-cost child care, and have a nurse on staff. The factory floor does not get too hot and there is natural light. The work there may come close to being meaningful.

These factories produce high-quality clothes that require no expensive rework and do not have flaws that would boomerang the clothes back from the customer to the point of purchase. They make clothes that one customer praises to another, which sustains the reputation for quality we prize most highly and would find most expensive to lose.

The next big task will be to secure a living wage for all workers making Patagonia goods. To be able to pay a living wage, factories will have to raise prices to avoid losing revenue, and thus risk worker lay-offs. Factories pay the same wages for similar work done for multiple brands, so the brands have to agree to pay more (a delicate step that opens companies to legal liability for price fixing).

Patagonia is currently working within the FLA toward a stepped approach to paying a living wage. But we also act on our own. We have begun to track the minimum and prevailing wage in each country from which we source and to negotiate something closer to a living wage with each factory. We would not have come to the decision to work toward paying a living wage in the supply chain had we not first undertaken, through the Footprint Chronicles, a self-examination of our labor practices. Any company can accomplish the same through conventional, but consistently transparent, CSR reporting. Whatever form it takes, transparency will benefit your company.

Several of our suppliers have been gratified to have their challenges brought before the consumer; they rarely get to tell the public the problems they experience and the work they are doing to improve the pay and working conditions of their people. As a result of the Footprint Chronicles, some suppliers have come to trust us more, share more information, and work more closely with us to solve mutual problems. This kind of collaboration makes our work feel meaningful to us.

As FLA has been an invaluable partner to help us improve social conditions in the supply chain, so Bluesign Technologies, an independent verification firm, has become our most important partner in the work to minimize environmental harm. Bluesign performs regular audits of members who agree to establish management systems to improve environmental performance in five key areas of the production process: resource productivity, consumer safety, water emissions,

{ 60 }

air emissions, and occupational health and safety. Members regularly report their progress and must meet improvement goals to maintain their status. It has been crucial for us to have systematic help to screen chemicals according to the following categories: blue, safe to use; gray, special handling required; and black, forbidden. Bluesign helps factories eliminate black chemicals and find equivalent alternatives.

The Bluesign standard is rigorous, and nine of our suppliers have now signed on. Currently Bluesign-approved fabrics comprise 30 percent of the total fabric used in Patagonia products. We have asked all our raw-materials suppliers to adopt the Bluesign standard by 2015.

The Footprint Chronicles have helped Patagonia remove barriers to improvements in quality as well as social and environmental conditions. These barriers can take the form of intransigence, cynicism, or indifference on the part of our suppliers and some of our own staff. But as the Chronicles have educated both our suppliers and ourselves, { 61 } we have made the choice to do better and not accept the status quo. This is how our work has become more meaningful: we're not just making clothes, we're making long-lasting clothes that do less damage.

Common Threads Initiative

The fabric analysis we commissioned during the early nineties, as a response to those employees who became sick in our Boston store, opened our eyes to the social and environmental cost of everything we made. If polyester proved to be a more benign fabric than chemically intensive cotton, it still came from oil drilled from the ground. If organic cotton was superior to its "conventional" counterpart, it still used water that drew down aquifers or relied on irrigation supported by a concrete dam that choked off the life of fish.

We began to consider the cradle-to-cradle thinking of architect William McDonough, who believes that just as natural waste regenerates life, human-made products at the end of their time should be remade into new products, preferably of equal value. We need to reduce reliance on scarce resources and keep our used-up products out of American landfills or European and Japanese incinerators.

With this in mind, in 2005 we initiated the Common Threads Recycling Program, inviting customers to send us their worn-out Capilene underwear, which we would send to our polyester supplier in Japan to melt down, then re-extrude as new fiber. By 2010 we intended to be able to take back any Patagonia product for recycling. Every season our intake of used Patagonia products increased. Over a six-year period we took in thirty-four tons of worn-out clothes for recycling or repurposing.

We have faced a number of challenges. In the best closed-loop system, as with our polyester underwear, the new fiber created from recycling the old maintains its value. But cotton and wool cannot be melted, only shredded, and the new fiber produced is not of equal value to the old. The coarse, short fibers of recycled cotton can be made into jeans or a thick, woodsman style shirt-jacket but not a fine woven shirt. Only one type of nylon, nylon 6, can be closed-loop recycled, and only with products made entirely of that fabric (e. g., boardshorts for surfers). We have to downcycle or shred most nylon clothes we make, including our expensive, technical waterproof jackets. We have not yet figured out how to recycle packs, although we have learned how to make handbags and wallets from used fishing waders and turn used wetsuits into beer koozies.

About halfway through our five-year stretch, we began to realize that, in spite of our progress, we were working backwards. No one should have to recycle what should never have been made. As environmental activist Annie Leonard has said, in the reduce, repair, reuse, recycle mantra, recycling comes last. If you want to reduce the environmental and social harm you do, the injunction to reduce comes first. Don't make what won't be useful or won't last. Don't buy what you don't need. But how do you continue to increase your sales if you ask your customers to reduce their consumption while you, like any other product-producing company, need three percent annual growth just to stay even?

Once we got past the flinching that comes naturally when you pursue an idea that threatens to put you out of business, we refashioned our recycling program as the Common Threads Initiative, a partnership with our customers to pursue the four classic Rs in their proper order.

We asked customers to pledge not to buy what they don't need or what won't last (if it's poorly made or likely to be fashionably wearable for only a season). We promised, in turn, to redouble our efforts to make useful, long-lasting products.

We asked customers to pledge to repair first, before discarding or replacing, what breaks. In turn, we upsized our repair department staff to get the work done and turned around more quickly. We asked customers to pledge to reuse or recirculate what they no longer wore. We set up a program with eBay to make it easier for customers to resell products and introduced used products for sale on our website. Would we lose business as a result? We wagered that if our customers were to buy more thoughtfully, and if we were to do our job well and make useful, high-quality products, they would continue to buy from us, and we'd gain new customers who shared our commitment.

In 2011, a year behind schedule, we began to accept the return of any worn-out Patagonia product ever made back for recycling or repurposing. And we added a fifth "r" to the mantra, to pledge mutually with the customer to reimagine a world in which we take from nature only what it can replace. This fifth "r" underpins the other four. If we don't keep the long view in mind, and close to hand, nature will cease to support our efforts to support ourselves.

Bill McKibben made an interesting point a few years back when he compared the yields of factory farming and low-input farming.

Subsidized factory farming yields more dollars per acre but a low-input (not necessarily organic) field yields more food. Factory farming requires industrial simplicity and heavy engineering: a few hundred acres of straight-rowed crops of the same variety, harvested by vehicles as expensive as Ferraris, fueled by copious amounts of oil. A farmer of ten acres, however, has to know and walk the land, and rely on intimate knowledge to tease out more of its productivity— to know where one plant thrives in another's shade, where to intercrop plants with roots of different lengths, and whether the earthworms are thriving. One type of farming exhausts the land, the other takes advantage of and takes part in the natural world.

We would argue that low-input, small-scale farming, more than the factory farm, represents sound business now and in the future. This is counterintuitive for those of us who grew up in the twentieth century, with its emphasis on streamlining and scalability. But the time has come for those of us in business to understand ourselves as a part of nature and to walk our fields; we need to make our practices less exhaustive and more intensive and productively alive, so that the world will be habitable for those who come after us.

Those of us who work have three large social roles to play. We are all citizens who cast our vote and lend our voice to what we want to see more of and less of in the world, and who reserve the right to both create and bring down governments.

We are all consumers, who can choose what we buy and, in aggregate, change the way corporations and ultimately governments behave.

We are also, in our working lives, producers. This is our most active public role. We have less control over what we do at work than in our personal lives and in the voting booth, but it is as producers that we make the biggest difference. Ninety percent of a product's environmental impact is committed at the design stage; two-thirds of waste is generated by industry, not households—so what we do at work has far greater consequence than going out on a Saturday morning to trade in the Hummer for a Prius. What we do at work every day matters.

Meaningful work: what is it exactly? Regardless of our talent or education; our preference for working with words, numbers, or our hands; our ability to cut a pattern, lay out an ad, or negotiate with a supplier, we have meaningful work at Patagonia because our company does its best to be responsible to nature and people. Our daily gestures—on the one hand, mundane and often tedious—are, on the other hand, infused with the effort to give something useful and enjoyable to society without bringing undue harm to nature, the commons, or other workers. Tedium is easier to take when it has meaning. To take one step toward responsibility, learn something, take another step, and let self-examination build on itself has engaged everyone at Patagonia. Many of our suppliers and customers are equally invested in this process of improvement. What engages us most deeply enlivens us. Lively, gratified workers make good business possible—make it thrive.

CHAPTER 5
THE ELEMENTS OF BUSINESS RESPONSIBILITY

{ 67 }

W<small>E'VE COME TO</small> the heart of our book, which is to lay out the elements of business responsibility, as we see them, to five key stakeholders: owners, workers, customers, communities, and nature. For each element we will provide, in an appendix, a related checklist of things companies can do to become more socially and environmentally responsible while strengthening their business health.

We have made the checklists available as a free download on Patagonia.com, in the form of an Excel sheet that you can edit and sort as appropriate to your own business and priorities. If you find our lists insufficient, search the internet for "Environmental Business Checklists," available from an array of local governments, NGOs and trade groups.

Two checklists we know and respect (and have used to help create our own) are: B Corporation's B Impact Assessment Tool (www.bcorporation.net) and Napa Green's (www.napagreen.org/downloads/ABAG_checklist.pdf) for wineries.

Where to start?

The answer depends on your role in your company. If you're not the CEO or don't have the power to establish a "corporate sustainability program," you can start anywhere. Check over the lists to see what you, in your particular company role, can do. It is a myth that taking better care of people and nature is at odds with business excellence. But what if your boss believes that? Concentrate on money-saving steps. No boss worth her stock options will stop you from saving the company money.

Or say you are a CEO. You want to go green. At least get greener. But as CEO you don't have the power this book's other readers might think you have. You have a board to answer to, nervous stockholders whose politics and level of environmental knowledge vary, a business climate that befuddles every tealeaf used in forecasting. You may rely on a CFO or COO who is convinced that climate change is a hoax, or damn well should be. How do you get him or her going? How do you bring along your people?

The best answer is to follow Daniel Goleman's creed: Know your impacts, favor improvement, share what you learn. As a method, these work in sequence: You have to know impacts before you can favor improvements before you can share what you've learned.

You can undertake your greening in three steps.

First, engage your team, with as broad participation as possible, to find out the worst things your company does, what costs you the most in reputation and profit, and what will be the easiest to correct. The easiest problems for your company to correct may seem complex and difficult to another, depending on the company's values and traits, and whether its cultural bias is for innovation or safety.

Address first what you suspect you know already; tease it out. What nags at you most whenever you hear about it (or see its consequences)? What is it you think you can do something about—that your company will be good at getting done? Ask your team to ask themselves the same questions.

Step two: Get together with your people to name your priorities for improvement, then winnow the list. Decide what you'll do first, how much time and money you'll spend on it, and how many people will be involved. Define what initial success will look like. Write that down on one page you can circulate among your team. Once you've figured out what improvements you want to make, where you can draw on your company's greatest strengths, take the fewest risks, save the most money, and create the most opportunity, go for it.

As you learn, share what you learn with as many people as possible in your organization, even if you don't think you (or they) have the time. Then share what you learn with stakeholders: suppliers, your trade association, key customers, even the key competitors you call on when you need to form a united front to get something done. Take advantage of the trust you earn, and you will earn more of it, especially if you are credible and tell the truth about your mistakes and failures; get going a little snowball of support.

Finally, using the trust you've deepened, the knowledge you've gained, and the confidence and pride that have built throughout the organization and among stakeholders, ask yourself: What does your company now know that enables you to take a next step that may have been out of reach before but suddenly lies within sight?

Keep going. Here's what will happen.

The company will get smarter, and more people will start to care deeply about creating a better-quality business through improving its social and environmental performance. In so doing, your people will *have* to pay better attention to all the business fundamentals—and this boost in applied intelligence will result in a more fluid, less wasteful organization. You will spot money leaks you could not see before, and you will gain the confidence to recognize and go after opportunities that a company bound by traditional corporate see-no-evil politesse cannot begin to address. Success motivates people, including your strays.

Doing good creates better business.

We know this from experience, both from our own years in business and from talking to others. Wal-Mart first had to learn how many millions of dollars it could save by eliminating unnecessary packaging for deodorant before it could adopt a long-term goal of zero waste. The company had to see how much environmental harm it could avoid and money it could save in single-stroke decisions before becoming more systematically responsible.

You may expect internal resistance at first, of course, depending on what you try to do, especially early on. The poet William Stafford once wrote that no poem should begin with a first line the reader can argue with. It distracts the person you want to reach. Get your people nodding in full agreement a few times before you say something that challenges the half-sleep of received wisdom.

A social and environmental initiative might start with something that unarguably needs doing. As they gain experience, your colleagues will become more aware of more nuanced, harder-to-spot social and environmental impacts, and of opportunities to reduce them. They will start to share a language and a cultural bias that favors improvement. Once an apparel manager at Wal-Mart hears the buzz on how much money the company has saved by eliminating packaging in one department, and how much more can be saved by similar measures, she will feel implicit permission to devote some time from her busy day to minimize packaging in her own part of the business. Managers often cling to the safety of familiar practices until they see their colleagues (and competitors within the company) dare to imagine, then implement, better practices. Courage can be contagious. So is success.

You'll need the support, early on, of company heroes at various levels in the hierarchy who are held in respect for their wisdom or competence or both. These heroes may not be among the company's most predictable advocates for social and environmental improvement—the 20 percent of us who sing in that choir. Expect and embrace surprising sources of collaboration, especially from thoughtful, often religiously motivated or stewardship-inspired conservatives, and for the collaborative process to change the company and everyone involved.

We underscore how critical it is for you to share what you learn as often and with as many as you can. Transparent social and environmental improvements will gradually increase your base of committed support within the company, from the margins (or the heights) to the center; any entrenched traditionalists gradually shuffle to the side, go elsewhere, or retire.

As your company comes to know more, and becomes confident enough to work cooperatively with outside partners to reduce environmental and social impacts, it will adopt that work permanently *as a part of doing business*. It becomes irresistible.

So you're not a CEO. Most consultants and experts we know argue that any major social and environmental initiative has to come top down, from the leadership. And of course no formal company initiative can succeed without top-down support or at least the absence of interference. Nevertheless, most fundamental changes start at the margins and move toward the center. And as long as reducing environmental harm, in particular, presents so many opportunities for companies to save money, or make money, you can't go wrong pursuing improvements from the bottom up, even in the employ of an uncongenial or unaware company.

Element #1: Responsibility to the Health of the Business

A company that aims to be socially and environmentally responsible has the same primary duty as any other business to know its numbers and pay its bills on time. A business cannot honor its social and environmental responsibilities unless it meets its first responsibility: to stay financially healthy.

But the means of measuring true business health is in its infancy. Accounting, as practiced, still assumes that the benefits of nature and the commons are free and that spoiling them has no cost. And, it's true, their loss doesn't show up on the books. But the loss or spoiling of natural systems and the commons entails huge costs for which people outside the company pay or suffer. Who shall be held accountable?

A movement has been afoot for several decades to persuade companies to take into account the value of nature and the commons. In 1994, consultant John Elkington coined the phrase "triple bottom line" (TBL), which measures indicators of social health (defined as human capital) and the planet (natural capital), as well as profit (capital). In 2007, the United Nations ratified TBL as a standard for public-sector accounting, as a means to measure the true cost of government subsidies to industry.

Two NGOs, The Nature Conservancy and Conservation International, are working with the accounting firm PriceWaterhouseCoopers to develop new methodologies to valuate ecosystems. As we mentioned in the first chapter, Dow Chemical has committed to invest $10 million over five years in partnership with The Nature Conservancy to develop strategies to price nature's unpaid work as a provider of biodiversity and "ecosystem services;" one-third of global food production, for example, relies on insect and animal pollination. Dow will use that information as a basis to evaluate the ecological costs of every business decision.

There also needs to be a better way to account for GDP that takes into account the resources of nature and the commons. New forms of social and environmental accounting may help discipline business away from our worst practices.

This is the idea behind a budding movement called Creating Shared Value (CSV). CSV argues for the interdependence of corporate success and the common good. It states that sustainable resources, educated workers, and consumers keep everything humming; they create wealth and pay taxes. Social responsibility should be integral to business strategy; the "value proposition" includes a social value proposition.

Hard to quarrel with that, or with Robert Zoellick, the president of the World Bank, who is starting a project to assign a dollar value to the natural capital of emerging and developing nations, because "the natural wealth of nations should be a capital asset, valued in combination with its financial capital, manufactured capital, and human capital." But note how chilling the language, and beware when everything under the sun folds inside the economic and political system and its powers. Assigning value to the priceless or quantifying the numberless presents risks of its own, similar to that of determining the quality of an education on the basis of test scores exclusively.

When money becomes the measure—as well as the means—of all things, the potential for economic and political mischief grows; there are no longer "externalities" outside the system to be left uncounted or ignored and let be. What are we to do, once we do these calculations, with wilderness? Wilderness doesn't really exist except as an idea—and, now, as a longing. We don't think a speech from John Muir on the need for ecosystem services would have swayed Teddy

Roosevelt to preserve Yosemite Park nearly as much as a night in the redwoods under the stars.

What citizens hold in common can not be free for the taking when there's no giving back. But not everything should have a price.

Element #2: Responsibility to the Workers

The Industrial Revolution, which has now extended its reach and introduced its system to most of the world, famously abstracts labor: the worker no longer owns his tools or her machines or bears full responsibility for the final product or necessarily knows the face of the man or woman who pays him and takes a share of his or her gain. And increasingly, companies rely less on people and more on robots to engage in large-scale manufacturing.

But by any standard, a company should do what it can to reward and care for the people who make its products and provide its services. All companies seeking to boost productivity need the loyalty, dedication, and creativity of their employees. The company's responsibility then extends to everyone in the supply chain who helps make or sell its product.

To fully engage the minds and hearts of employees, and minimize both the balk and bulk associated with bureaucracy, larger companies have to figure out how to best organize productive working groups of different sizes for different ends. Twelve is a good number for a small group to bond and work in concert to achieve a specific task with minimum hierarchy (think of a jury, a tribal hunting party, or an army squad). Anthropologist Robin Dunbar cites 150 as the magic number for community cohesion, based on the number of human relationships the human brain can handle. When it builds a new plant, the manufacturer W. L. Gore puts in 150 parking spaces. When the plant exceeds that capacity, the company builds a new one. Microsoft and Intel also limit the number of employees per building to 150, though they both

{ 74 }

run plants with multiple buildings. Hutterites form a new community when they reach that number. Along the same lines, a military company comprises between 80 and 225 people.

At Patagonia we've noticed changes in cohesion when we move different departments to different floors and buildings. Adjacency and proximity matter: to have our environmental team next door to the CEO engendered a certain dynamic; the CEO at the time became an environmental enthusiast. When the enviros moved to Marketing, they found new allies through daily contact with the people who tell the company's stories.

A department can have only so many immediate neighbors at one time. People at Patagonia form important cross-departmental friendships and garner cross-departmental intelligence in our café, on lunchtime runs, and among fellow parents of kids in childcare. It's important to create comfortable spaces throughout the plant for {75} employees to gather in small groups of two and three, as well as more formal meeting rooms.

Chouinard Equipment, Patagonia's predecessor, was, as we mentioned, curiously pre-Industrial Revolution. Our tin sheds held equipment: a drop-hammer forge, an anvil, a coal forge, jigs for drilling aluminum chocks, but no time clocks or assembly lines. Everyone was poor and most lived marginal, if well-traveled, lives. For a while we paid a 10 percent bonus to anyone who had the initiative to work forty hours a week, a practice that turned out to be illegal; we were busted and required to stop. We partied heartily; the sheds faced a courtyard where we celebrated almost any event with an asado of barbecued lamb and a keg.

When we became a clothing company, and as sales increased, we had to become more professional, a process that at first consisted of throwing bright, inexperienced young people into new jobs to see if they could learn what we needed to know how to do.

We paid fairly well, considering the inexperience of our employees. Early on we provided health care, although we did not have to. We have told the story of how we introduced childcare and parental leave. We never made anyone "dress" for work (though those coming into the company from the workaday world had to re-learn how to dress casually in order to fit in). People were free to take a long break mid-day to go surf or run, with the understanding that they came in early or stayed late—at any rate, got the work done.

Our worst day as an employer came in 1991, when we laid off 150 employees. For two years we had managed the company too carelessly, bought too much inventory, sold too little of it, hired too many people, and salted away too little money to pay for an expansion that our bank cheerfully financed until they got into troubles of their own and pulled the plug. Costs had to go down and fast. After weeks of considering alternatives (like a shorter work week, combined with a cut in pay), we decided to let go of 20 percent of our people—and all on the same morning to reduce the duration of the toxic atmosphere that persists when layoffs are expected. A consultant advised us how to handle the logistics: all day long employees watched their colleagues get called out for a talk and return without a job. By ten o'clock, employees had started to recoil, to roll back in their chairs, at the sight of a manager re-entering the room to approach the desk of yet another fellow worker.

Our emergency plan for a downturn of any magnitude now is to cut the fat, freeze hiring, reduce travel, and trim every type of expense except salaries and wages. We've done this for short periods several times—once right after 9/11. If things get worse, eliminate bonuses, which we once did. We paid them retroactively the following year, when the picture got brighter. Worse still, and decisions get tougher. Half of our expenses are labor. Before we would cut anyone else's pay, we would reduce the salaries of managers, directors, vice-presidents, and the top executives, including the owners. Then we would shorten the work week and reduce pay accordingly. Only as a last resort, if we were in the deepest sort of trouble, would we again downsize the company with a general layoff.

We should note the bracing fact that in 1991, after the layoffs, morale improved among the workers still with us. The hovering axe had fallen; those of us left still had our necks. We were a much soberer lot, absent the intoxication of growth, and more focused. We knew what we had to do to bring the business back to financial health, and we did.

Element #3: Responsibility to Your Customers

How to gain a customer and keep one? First, make something or offer a service someone can use, for which satisfaction endures. Second, your company should romance, but not bullshit, the people whose business it solicits.

Paul Hawken, when he was still running his Smith & Hawken gardening supplies company, told us that he didn't like to advertise because he didn't want that kind of relationship with his customers. He was referring to the alternate-reality environment of the magazine ad, wherein a business bullhorns its message in the same space as other unrelated voices all barking their own individual messages—like a bazaar but without the smell of spices or the dance of a charmed snake.

Since the mid-1980s, when Hawken made his comment, commercial space has much expanded and grown ever more noisy. More products have become more disposable; more customers experience more frustration when a flimsy product fails, and they have to deal with the customer-service person on the scratchy line from the offshore call center, who has no authority to correct a problem and, instead, didactically repeats the company's rules.

If the chase for cheaper labor is playing out to its conclusion, so is the race to attract customers on price alone, when the product in question won't last and the service won't deliver. Any customer can go online and find the cheapest price for anything, anywhere in the world. And any customer dissatisfied with a product or service can post it to a blog. So can any customer who questions the way a chicken has been raised or a sweatshirt sewn.

The strongest thing your company can do is something no one else will do, or do well.

To turn for a moment to romance: Selling and marketing seek to incite desire, but a company has to love to sell something its customer loves to buy. For both ethical and practical reasons, the selling story, to paraphrase Mark Twain, has to be mostly true. A company needs to present itself well to the customer; it may even preen a little, the way a lover might take care to dress for a date. A life story, or product story, told just this side of myth-making is okay when it fairly represents the real. But beware of conjuring a false image of your company's goods or services. Mystification will no longer work in a world where stage fog can be quickly dispersed by a competitor, activist, or regulator.

If you are responsible for a company's advertising and marketing, be truthful. The anonymous, sonorous talking head doesn't really represent your brand or product. Neither does Tiger Woods. Most people under forty don't watch the ads placed on TV at such great expense; they fast-forward through the boring bits when they watch the show after airtime on a laptop. They get their news from Jon Stewart and then Twitter it to their friends. And they have been raised to be concerned about the fate of the planet and want to support companies that are responsible.

Customers are expensive to find and to replace; they will become more so. The responsible company has to treat the customer as, if not a friend, a neighbor or colleague who shares a love of what the company offers, say a particular kind of clothing, food, shelter, education, art, sport, or entertainment. The wooing of customers can be assigned a cost per thousand exposures, scaled, tested, subjected to strategy. But the relationship, once sealed, is intimate and cannot be abstracted or reduced to a transaction. Someone will be happy to get your company's email or he may wince; she will order from your catalog or use it as kindling.

The duration of the relationship is contingent on the company's ability to provide more things the customer needs and on the customer's continued confidence in the company. The responsible company has to continue to state its case: provide the best information it can on why its products or services meet a need, how those products are made, how long they'll last, what the customer has to do to make them last longer with less environmental impact and, finally, what to do with them when they reach the end of their useful life.

A business has a responsibility to inform the customer of the environmental and social choices embodied in a product or service, from the time of purchase forward.

Element #4: Responsibility to the Community

Every company has a responsibility to its community, which includes the neighborhoods and cities in which we operate, its varied communities of interest, and the virtual community of blogs and social media.

Responsible companies have long supported their communities' hospitals, schools, and arts organizations. The best companies have also recognized their significance to the economic health of their communities and have avoided closing plants when possible, or have helped soften the impact of a closing by phasing out rather than shutting down production, offering generous severance pay to laid-off workers, and supporting the community institutions that aid the unemployed.

For 200 years, cities and neighborhoods have been vulnerable to the instabilities of capitalism. Its siren songs lure the peasantry from the countryside with a promise of wealth, but deliver instead, especially for that first generation off the farm, hard urban poverty. A rise in the standard of living for one generation is no guarantee for the next.

The rising tide may lift boats, but it can also flood neighborhoods, leaving hardship in its wake. The current sinking of the middle class, especially in the United States, where the social safety net has been knit more loosely than in Europe and Japan, is strikingly evident in the landscape. In the United States of 2012, as this book is being written, we have two extremes with little in between: there are nearly abandoned Midwestern towns and dilapidated American city centers on the one hand and, on the other, zip codes where the restaurant with a hot new chef offers thousand-dollar wines and families of four live in houses big enough for twenty. *The Wall Street Journal* has reported that income disparity in the United States now approaches that of Mexico or the Philippines. Procter & Gamble, one of the last mass marketers, now has to pitch its products high or low; not enough people are left in the middle to matter.

What businesses do to their communities matters. Citizens from Palo Alto or Greenwich to Detroit or Smyrna, Tennessee, are directly hurt or helped by the decision made by companies with a local presence to put down roots or pull out. (We were not popular in Bozeman, Montana, when we pulled up stakes to move our call center to Reno.)

Every company needs to ask itself: If you do business around the world, where are you local? And what are your obligations to those places you call home?

Home is wherever you have a concentration of employees, as we do in Ventura, Reno, Kamakura (Japan) and Annecy (France) and, to a lesser extent, wherever we have stores. We help make each store local in part by giving it an annual budget for grants to local environmental groups, with recipients determined by employee vote. Although we are not a significant employer for any community, except perhaps

Ventura (workforce, 350; county population, 825,000), we are mindful of how what we do affects local housing, traffic, infrastructure, and habitat. As well as maintaining relationships with local environmental groups, we participate in beach and creek cleanups and habitat restoration.

Reducing travel is an environmental necessity that, in the long run, will affect business communities. At Patagonia we rely on extensive business travel to maintain our relationships with satellite operations, suppliers, and customers, as well as the industry organizations with whom we work to reduce our environmental impact. Our business assumes, and depends on, the mobility of our customer base. But air travel will become increasingly expensive, as it should; for while it conserves time, or used to, it wastes an astonishing amount of fuel on a passenger-per-mile basis. One solution is to cluster operations geo-graphically, wherever possible. Companies need to undertake separate manufacturing steps in geographically proximate factories, and to ship from a port as close as possible to the final assembly point. Note that travel by rail or cargo ship is relatively environmentally benign on a per-product basis. We cause more environmental harm trucking a jacket on the short, final leg from the port in L.A. to the warehouse in Reno than we do shipping the same product across the breadth of the Pacific.

{ 81 }

The task for all of us during the next half-century will be to scale the industrial model down rather than up. There are strong reasons to decentralize the energy grid so that when a crow fries a transformer in Alberta it doesn't silence a sound stage in L.A. There is no reason to believe that the monoculture created by business activity is any healthier for economic life than agricultural monoculture is for the health of ecosystems.

Element #5: Responsibility to Nature

The business world needs to see the economic and environmental equivalent of the astronomic truth that the earth rotates around a sun, and that the universe does not radiate out in a flat plane from the earth. That truth is this: Our economy depends on nature, not the other way around, and companies will destroy the economy if they destroy nature.

We know that we are not superior to nature, but our language says otherwise. We refer to nature as "resources," as though nature were here to be at our disposal. We refer to nature as our "environment," as though nature were here to wrap itself around us. We refer to ourselves as "stewards," as though God had ordained us to be nature's keeper, a big key dangling from our neck, a white towel slung over the arm.

Our first responsibility is to be more humble, and yet also more confident. We are a part of nature; we *can* learn to live on our planet without spoiling it.

Our second responsibility is to, whenever and wherever we can, leave nature be. We all know when we see a patch of land that should be left wild or a stretch of water that should be freed from the chokehold of a dam that has outlived its purpose. We need to restore the natural systems with which we've tampered. Nature has immense restorative powers, once the sources of assault are removed.

Our third responsibility, as we have argued throughout this book, is to reduce the harm we do in the course of ordinary business and take birth-to-rebirth responsibility for what we make or bears our name.

A few quick, practical tips before you consult our five checklists in the appendix: ·

Remember that 90 percent of a product's environmental impact is determined at the design stage. Life-cycle analysis, the most critical tool for learning everything that goes into making your product, is expensive and time consuming, especially for smaller companies with limited resources. Therefore, it's best to measure what is most important and what you can do something about: the 80/20 rule applies. If 20 percent of your products generate 80 percent of your sales, analyze those products to gauge the lion's share of your impact. Moreover, if possible, work with an industry organization with a sharable methodology, database, and software that enable you to capture the necessary social and environmental data as part of your ordinary reporting systems.

We intend our checklists as points of departure. They give you an idea of the range of what can be done to make a difference—from removing the water pipe of a urinal to using recycled wallboard to taking back your used-up products to be recycled. Start with some kind of assessment of what you presently do to minimize your energy and water use and waste. Adapt the checklists to your priorities. Figure out what can be done most easily and least expensively (or to produce the most savings), and with the least resistance.

But it's also worthwhile to look at what seems most difficult and far-fetched. What seems hardest to do, or boldest, may be precisely what you need to do to motivate others, including customers and competitors, as well as suppliers, to join you in your efforts. Checking off the easy stuff gives us experience and builds confidence. Tackling the big stuff, and surviving setbacks and failures, makes us smarter, stronger, and more useful to others. Doing both can lead to environmental and social gains of the sort we need: some wildly imaginative, some quietly effective, some both. It will take all kinds of work to repair the damage.

CHAPTER 6
SHARING KNOWLEDGE

Transparency is the primary contemporary virtue for all responsible businesses. It is crucial to share knowledge within the company so that social and environmentally responsible behavior can be mandated as part of every job. No business can afford to create a separate environmental bureaucracy or burden its human-resources staff with a host of new responsibilities. Everyone in a company must help. To do so, they need a broad and detailed picture of the company's social and environmental footprint. For a company to set goals or assess progress toward meeting them it needs freely flowing, transparent information. No transparency: no accountability.

Every company will also have to involve outsiders in its quest to become more responsible, to share information with—and tap information from—customers, suppliers, competitors, standards-setting organizations, independent monitors, and so on. Companies rightly guard certain information: patentable technology, business-development strategy, the mysterious Indian Ocean island source for the vanilla in the cookie batter. But much of what companies hold secret would be better off revealed. Your factory list? Why not publish it? To publish your factory list lends your competitors, who may be less bold than you, a new, adoptable "best practice"; this, in turn, permits them to publish their own factory list.

An increase in transparency makes it easier for competitors to work co-operatively to solve problems that range from materials shortages to emissions and effluents to the need for a better grievance process for the workers on the floor. The more you reveal about your environmental and social environmental challenges and successes, the more you help others in your industry who are trying to reduce their social and environmental footprint. When it comes to protecting nature and human beings from harm, we are all on the same side.

It makes sense, moreover, for companies to organize themselves into industry-wide working groups to develop a shared methodology. These groups, with the help of an independent monitoring firm, can compare data and cooperate on improvements. In the two industry groups with which we have been involved (the OIA's Eco Working Group and the Sustainable Apparel Coalition), the level of trust among the participating companies has increased, making communication easier. During the past two years, both groups have become more ambitious and have strengthened, rather than diluted, their common social and environmental standards. Trust among colleagues has not been achieved simply because we all set out to be more virtuous. Our collaborative work to develop the indexes signals a confluence of virtue and perceived opportunity.

It makes sense, too, for suppliers to work together to better identify their common problems and priorities. When Wal-Mart wanted to
make more systematic improvements and implement its goal of 100
percent renewable energy use, zero waste, and products "that sustain
our resources and the environment," it went to its suppliers for help.
Wal-Mart had discovered that only 10 percent of its environmental
impact came from store operations and transportation, whereas 90
percent lay in the supply chain. They realized they couldn't understand the harm done in their company's name without a thorough
understanding of the conditions in which their products were made
and the processes used to make them. The removal of packaging and
installation of power units for the truck fleet meant little compared to
what could be accomplished in the supply chain to reduce energy use,
water use, and waste.

We are entering a post-consumerist society because the economy
based on consumption has outgrown itself and its rationale—it no longer provides enough good jobs and it poisons the well. The principled
work being done by responsible industry groups is the harbinger of an
economy that might replace it: one that better meets the deeper needs of
human beings *and* gives nature and the commons a rest from onslaught.

Perhaps that paints too blue a sky.

Let's return one last time to our own story. Patagonia was not
always an especially transparent company, nor were we eager to learn
about problems that seemed beyond our control. We collectively
groaned when we learned how harmful conventionally grown cotton
was. We had no idea when we decided to switch to organic cotton how
much work would be involved; we knew only that it was possible, and
that we had no compelling reason to continue to use harmful, chemically dependent cotton.

When we agreed to be a member of President Clinton's task force on sweatshop labor, we didn't really know if we were in the clear ourselves. We wiped the fog from our lens only with the assistance of an independent verification service, the Fair Labor Association, which grew out of the presidential task force. We couldn't do everything alone. No one can. Sometimes what we need to know is beyond us: we have textile scientists on staff, but we could not possibly garner within our company the necessary knowledge of chemicals and toxins to conduct our own audits of dyehouses and fiber manufacturers. It has been invaluable to team with Bluesign Technologies, which does have the necessary expertise.

Our effort at transparency began gingerly. But soon enough, the Footprint Chronicles put our feet to the fire. Take Arvind, a large vertical supplier in India that contracts with cooperatives of organic-cotton farmers, then spins and sews the cotton into jeans in their own factories. When we began to work with Arvind, we violated one of our own rules, which obliges us to visit a factory to do a social audit before we place the first order. We had our excuses: our director of social responsibility had left the company; our new director had not yet arrived, and Arvind had an excellent reputation. So we punted. When our new director made the trip, after production had already begun, she found several violations of our Code of Conduct, some small, some major, some cultural: flip flops worn around chemicals; no railing around a wastewater pool; a first-aid cabinet locked to prevent theft of its supplies. We met with Arvind and said we wanted to discuss this visit on our website and work with them to solve the violations over time. They agreed.

It has improved the quality of our clothing to have it sewn by people who are decently treated by managers held accountable for their behavior. By examining our supply chain, we got to know our suppliers better; because we learned what our suppliers do, how they do it, and the specific challenges of their work, they trust us more. We now solve problems of any kind with them more quickly. Our transparency illustrates the seriousness of our standards to our suppliers. Last, but certainly not least, it deepens our customers' knowledge of what they buy.

Customers, who in recent years have begun to pay far more attention to what they spend, will increasingly want to know whether the person who assembled your product was paid fairly and works in safe conditions. They will want to know whether your product is worth the air it has polluted. Before they buy, customers increasingly will rate your own social and environmental standards and performance against that of your competition.

Transparency is a precondition of positive change but does not guarantee it. When we developed a group of well-made, durable new daypacks, they sold like hotcakes. Yet we knew we had cut environmental corners to shave cost to meet the price we thought would generate strong sales and sufficient profit. We used no recycled fabrics in these packs, as had been our custom. So we said all this on our website. The result? No customers have complained, sales have remained brisk, and our designers, though ashamed of themselves, have yet to come up with a more environmentally friendly fabric that performs equally well. Transparency may hold feet to the fire but doesn't always toast the soles; the experience of shame doesn't always change behavior.

Transparency clears the ground for doing good and, in our experience, more often than not creates some momentum for it, absent overwhelming obstacles. The perceived loss of a profit center can be one such obstacle. To improve the environmental quality of Patagonia's daypack fabric will require from our designers what transparency does not automatically provide: a fresh infusion of persistence, and imagination to instill environmental value into these packs without sacrificing revenue. That will be hard to do. But the advantage of transparency is to make clear what has to be done.

THE RESPONSIBLE COMPANY

CHAPTER 7
WHERE TO FROM HERE?

Doing the right thing usually emboldens people to do more of the right thing.

Companies that recognize the opportunity to use the intelligence and creative capacity of their people to do less harm, certainly less harm that serves no useful purpose, will benefit. The company that wreaks less environmental harm will at the same time reduce its sharply rising costs for energy, water, and waste disposal.

Smaller companies can latch onto the efforts of bigger companies, yet dare to do what bigger companies may not be limber enough to do. Bigger companies can accomplish big things; harm done on an industrial scale has to be reduced on an industrial scale.

We advocate a combination of steady improvements with the occasional, breathtakingly bold move to keep everyone awake and motivated, to show leadership that reflects well on everyone in the company. Bold moves that disrupt accepted practices are more likely to lead to the discovery of a new, more environmentally responsible product or service you can offer.

No one needs to sit out the dance. Even if you work in a conservative company, ask yourself, what are my social and environmental responsibilities and possibilities here? Do the best you can to act on them.

The environmental crisis has arrived in tandem with a crisis of labor. The advanced industrial economies no longer create enough well-paying jobs; the job base no longer underpins, with any stability, the economy. We need a new economy built on smaller-scale enterprise, more attentively managed and more environmentally responsible, and we have no time to lose.

There is much to be done, and much we can do. Start where you get the least resistance and most cooperation: go on from there. Work with everyone you can, including competitors.

How will you know if you're on track? Over time, your company will become healthier as a benefit of knowing your business more intimately—and more fully engaging your workforce and community. You'll know you're on track whenever you ask yourself and your colleagues, Why didn't we do this sooner?

WHERE TO FROM HERE?

THE
CHECKLISTS

W<small>E CANNOT MAKE</small> these checklists comprehensive because many companies use specialized equipment and all have needs particular to their enterprise or business culture. We have tried to err, however, on the side of mundane detail. To make a policy targeting energy use over multiple years is good. But the policy itself won't switch out your lightbulbs.

No company on earth can check off every item on the lists below. It might be helpful to check off what your company does do now. You will then be aware of what needs to be done, plan your progress, then track it.

FINANCIAL BASICS FOR A COMPANY OF ANY SIZE:

☐ Maintain a board of directors that meets regularly, has at least one independent outside member, and oversees executive compensation.

☐ Share financial information with all employees; no one should be innumerate.

☐ Have financial controls in place to prevent fraud.

☐ Have financial reports reviewed by the board of directors and audited by an independent accounting firm.

☐ Incorporate into the mission statement a commitment to reducing social and environmental harm.

☐ Share information with stakeholders on reducing social and environmental harm.

☐ Provide employee training to reduce social and environmental harm.

☐ Dedicate, even if part-time, staff to monitor the company's social and environmental performance.

PAY, BENEFITS, AND POLICIES FOR COMPANIES OF ANY SIZE:

Pay a living wage; if you can't, figure out when you can.

Determine whether your company pays above-market, at-market, or below-market rates. Paying below market means your competitors will attract the best talent, including your own.

Calculate the multiple by which the company's highest paid employee compares to its lowest-paid full-time worker. Set a goal over a specific period of time to narrow the gap to a specific multiple, appropriate to your industry.

{ 97 }

Calculate your average annual attrition rate and compare with that of other employers in your business. If your number doesn't look good, figure out why. Set a bench-mark for improvement.

Calculate the internal hire rate for open positions. If you have to hire outside too often, are you training properly and allowing people to grow in their jobs?

Include as many employees as possible in the company's bonus plan to secure broad-based support for company goals.

In countries without national insurance, like the U.S., offer health insurance to all half-time and full-time employees.

- Make health insurance available at cost to employees' families and domestic partners. Offer flexible spending accounts (FSA).

- Make available a 401(k) pension or equivalent plan for all employees after six months on the job.

- Contribute generously to the 401(k) pension plan to encourage employee participation.

- Diversity and gender balance, at all levels of the workforce, are strong virtues in a workforce; discourage both management myopia and provincialism.

- Provide stock options or equivalent forms of company ownership to as broad a base of employees as possible. (Note: Patagonia doesn't offer stock options. Having investigated employee ownership, Yvon and Malinda Chouinard, the owners, are concerned that, with shares more broadly distributed, the company would become overly cautious about undertaking risk in the pursuit of its environmental goals. So that Patagonia can continue to push back the boundaries of what businesses consider possible, Yvon and Malinda are willing to undertake risks that might give pause to a broader ownership, even of employees committed to reducing environmental impact.)

- Provide generous vacation pay: one week after six months employment; two weeks after one year; three and four weeks as soon as possible.

- Provide paid sick leave and personal days, including bereavement leave, and days to care for sick children.

- Provide paid maternity and paternity leave for at least 90 days.

- Allow part-time and flextime and telecommuting opportunities as appropriate.

- Install showers so employees can exercise at lunch or bike to work.

- Establish a relationship with a good childcare center close to work.

- Ensure that facilities meet Occupational Safety and Health Administration (OSHA) standards or international equivalent.

- Ensure that facilities meet Americans with Disabilities Act (ADA) standards or international equivalent.

{ 99 }

PAY, BENEFITS, AND POLICIES FOR COMPANIES WITH 50 OR MORE EMPLOYEES:

- Offer supplemental disability insurance to full-time employees and dental and vision insurance to full-time or long-term employees.

- Provide a company café or kitchen or, if not practical, a dedicated space to let employees eat and/or rest.

- Provide on-site day care if possible (or establish a relationship with a local provider).

- Maintain a board of directors that meets regularly, has at least one independent outside member, and oversees executive compensation.

- Share financial information with all employees; no one should be innumerate.

- Have financial controls in place to prevent fraud.

- Have financial reports reviewed by the board of directors and audited by an independent accounting firm.

- Incorporate into the mission statement a commitment to reducing social and environmental harm.

- Share information with stakeholders on reducing social and environmental harm.

- Provide employee training to reduce social and environmental harm.

- Dedicate, even if part-time, staff to monitor the company's social and environmental performance.

- Subsidize employee travel to work by public transportation or walking/biking to minimize carbon impact of commuting.

- Provide paid or subsidized training opportunities for a broad base of employees.

- Provide paid week- to month-long internship opportunities for individual employees to offer their skills to nonprofit organizations in alignment with the company's mission.

- Provide paid sabbatical leave for long-term managerial and creative staff to help prevent burnout.

- Pay severance to nonexecutive employees who depart in good standing after two years, and specify the amount as a percentage of salary in the employee handbook.

- Get rid of dehumanizing cubicles; let there be natural light.

COMMUNICATION FOR COMPANIES OF ANY SIZE:

- Publish an employee handbook that details the company's mission as well as its benefits and expectations. It should include a Code of Ethics, antidiscrimination/harassment policies, and a policy that enables employees to register grievances without fear of reprisal.

- On an annual basis, conduct a job-satisfaction survey of all employees; quantify and share the results.

- Require that supervisors write an annual performance appraisal for their staff. Supervisors should consult employees' co-workers and key contacts within the company, set goals (including social and environmental performance goals) for the coming year, and determine training needs.

- In a manufacturing or warehouse facility, track all injuries and time lost to injuries.

POLICIES FOR COMPANIES OF ANY SIZE:

☐ Make long-lasting products whose parts can be repaired.

☐ Make useful things that have an identifiable benefit to the user.

☐ Make things that benefit the commons.

☐ Make things that benefit health or healthy activities (e.g. organic food, mountain bikes, etc.).

☐ Make things that benefit artistic or scientific activity, e.g. pianos or astrolabes.

☐ Make things that are multifunctional.

☐ Vigilantly avoid unnecessary product proliferation (including excessive options, whether of colors or accessories, for popular products).

☐ Make environmentally preferable substitutes for environmentally harmful products.

☐ Have production or manufacturing processes screened by a third party (e.g., Forest Stewardship Council (FSC), Bluesign Technologies, or LEED) to reduce environmental harm.

☐ Be progressively transparent about the social and environmental impact of what you make. Is anyone in your industry working on a manufacturer- or brand-facing index? Participate.

☐ Guarantee your product unconditionally.

{ 102 }

☐ Serve the underserved; donate what you no longer need to those who do. It may even get your company a tax break.

LOCAL INVOLVEMENT FOR BUSINESSES OF ANY SIZE:

☐ Bank locally where possible—where they know you and you know them.

☐ Make opportunities available for lower-income people in your community.

☐ Where possible, provide work for those with physical or learning disabilities.

☐ Establish a community service policy. Benchmark and measure performance.

☐ Encourage employees to organize group volunteer activities.

☐ Create partnerships with local organizations that benefit the environment and the commons.

☐ Make your facilities available for use by local organizations outside your working hours.

☐ Make opportunities available for lower-income people in your community.

If possible, create a charitable foundation; if your company is too small to do that, give in ways that will make a difference for the communities or causes your company cares about most.

Have your charitable giving certified by 1% for the Planet or another branded organization that promotes and vets charitable giving.

YOUR COMMUNITY SUPPLIERS

Identify the major suppliers that represent 80 percent of your purchases. Meet with them annually to mutually review the quality and success of the relationship.

Create and maintain an ethics policy for transacting with suppliers.

Communicate to your suppliers, in writing, and in person, your company's mission, including your social and environmental standards.

Write a code of conduct that identifies your social and environmental standards; insist that your suppliers post your code of conduct where people do significant work on your company's behalf.

Set social and environmental standards for your major suppliers.

Have third-party services verify whether and how those standards are met. If they are not, but your supplier is operating in good faith, set goals for continuous improvement in social, environmental, and quality performance;

the goals should reflect mutual effort. Benchmark and evaluate performance.

☐ Share with other companies what you learn when improving social and environmental performance so that your industry can follow your lead in establishing best practices.

☐ Encourage major suppliers to use renewable energy and to target and track usage.

☐ Encourage major suppliers to reduce and monitor greenhouse gas emissions.

☐ Encourage major suppliers to reduce waste and divert it from landfill and incinerators and benchmark and track progess.

☐ Encourage major suppliers to benchmark and reduce water use (and to recirculate or recover water).

☐ Mandate the use of wastewater recovery systems by major suppliers.

☐ Work with appropriate trade associations to set standards for your industry that reduce social and environmental harm, and to educate consumers to the impacts of the products they buy.

This list is extensive, though not exhaustive, in order to benefit as many companies as possible, whether agricultural, administrative, or industrial. We have organized the list by the following categories: general and design tips; reduction of energy, water, waste and toxics; tips for construction, offices, lunchrooms, and landscaping.

We have attempted to minimize repetition, but some items will of necessity appear in more than one category.

GENERAL TIPS:

☐ Conduct independent (if possible) audits of energy and water use, and waste generation. Your utility companies might be helpful.

☐ Inventory carbon use.

☐ For energy, water, and carbon use, and waste generation, target and measure reductions.

☐ Share both targets and results with your board of directors, employees, and other businesses engaged in related activities. Do this in staff meetings, company newsletters, suggestion and reward programs, employee manual, and new-hire orientations.

☐ Work with your major suppliers, business partners and customers to reduce the environmental impact of activity done in your name. (You can use as a departure point a life-cycle analysis of the 20 percent of your products that generate 80 percent of your sales.)

- Dedicate a small staff to serve as an environmental resource for business and operational units. Do not create an environmental bureaucracy. Do not subordinate the environmental department to a public-relations or marketing arm of the company. Better that your enviros come out of UC Davis than Ogilvy Mather.

- Incorporate environmental goals into job descriptions and performance appraisals, as appropriate.

- Perform as soon as possible a life-cycle assessment (LCA) of the products that constitute 80 percent of your business.

- Conduct an independent audit of the toxicity of the major materials used in your products and manufacturing processes—or hire an independent organization like Bluesign, which can work directly with your suppliers.

- Benchmark and target increases in the use of recycled and biodegradable materials; measure performance.

- Benchmark and target reductions in packaging.

- Conduct an independent audit of transportation for all inbound freight. Use less air and truck shipping, more rail and ocean freight. Increase your efficiency; reduce energy use and pollution.

- Work with your industry trade associations to establish tools that can be integrated into your IT software to measure environmental impact and help improve performance.

- Take back worn-out products for recycling or repurposing or work with a partner to do so.

- Design products to be of high quality and lasting value—and with repairable components. The greenest product is often the one the customer doesn't have to replace.

- Design products to serve as many uses as possible (think cast-iron pan v. electric can opener).

- Design products to include as much recycled material as possible.

- Design products that wear out evenly and whose components can easily be replaced, so that the whole product does not need to be thrown away when a single part fails.

- Design products that can be recycled and, when possible, into products of equal value. (Better that synthetic underwear becomes new underwear, not carpet backing).

- Design products with minimal packaging.

ENERGY REDUCTION
GENERAL TIPS

- Monitor energy bills for spikes in use that may indicate the need for maintenance.

- Buy renewable energy credits from Bonneville Environmental Foundation (www.b-e-f.org) to offset greenhouse gas emissions from company travel and energy use.

- Purchase renewable energy from your utility company.

TRAVEL AND COMMUTING

- Reduce corporate travel.

- Set standards for corporate travel. Define priorities for types of business travel from highest to lowest. First- and business-class travel skyrocket the passenger-per-mile environmental cost.

- Establish videoconferencing facilities; ensure that they work properly and that employees are trained in their use.

- Convert your fleet to natural gas-powered or low-emissions vehicles.

- Create a vanpool program if possible.

- Encourage employees to take the bus or train, carpool, or bicycle or walk to work.

- Subsidize these alternative transportation methods, if possible.

- Post to your intranet carpool ride sign-up sheets, bicycle-route maps, and mass-transit schedules/maps.

- Offer telecommuting opportunities and flexible schedules.

- Offer lockers and showers for staff who bicycle to work.

- Provide secure bicycle storage for staff and customers.

- Provide loaner bikes so employees can do chores or go to doctor appointments without bringing in their cars.

Offer electric vehicle recharge ports for visitors and staff using electric vehicles.

Make your facility a Zipcar site, so people who need a car for an errand don't have to drive into work.

HEATING AND AIR CONDITIONING

A simple tune-up can increase the energy efficiency of your furnace by 5 percent and you can save up to 10 percent by insulating and tightening up ventilation ducts.

Use ceiling fans rather than central A/C units: they use 98 percent less energy.

Heat with natural gas, which can be up to 55 percent more efficient than electricity.

Install renewable energy sources, such as solar panels or wind generators.

Use a 365-day programmable thermostat to control heating and air conditioning.

Install a geothermal heat pump in appropriate climates.

Install double-pane windows where appropriate.

Supplement A/C systems with evaporative coolers on condensers.

Use economizers on A/C to increase air circulation.

Replace a single or package A/C unit with one that exceeds Title 24 building standards.

- [ ] Use CO_2 occupancy sensors to control air conditioning and heat. These can be found online at relatively low cost.

- [ ] Provide shade for HVAC condenser, especially for rooftop fixtures.

- [ ] Shade sun-exposed windows and walls: use awnings, sunscreens, shade trees or shrubbery.

- [ ] Apply window film to reduce solar heat gain on clear, single-pane, non-northern facing windows.

- [ ] Set thermostat to 78° F for cooling, 68°F for heating and use the thermostat's night setback. If you don't control the temperature, talk to whoever pays the bill. Circulate a letter to everyone sharing the system to suggest how much money could be saved.

- [ ] Seal off unused areas. Block and insulate unneeded windows and other openings.

- [ ] Use small fans or a space heater during off hours instead of cooling or heating the entire office.

- [ ] Complete regularly scheduled maintenance on HVAC and refrigeration systems at least twice a year. Change filters every two months to optimize performance and extend equipment life. Clean entire systems each year and check for coolant leaks, duct sealing, clogs, and obstructions of air intake and vents. Clean condenser coils of dust and lint and evaporator coils of excessive frost. Inspect and repair economizers on AC systems.

- [ ] Use weather stripping (weatherizing and caulking) to seal air gaps around doors and windows.

{ 111 }

Insulate all hot water pipes.

Use instantaneous hot water heaters at point of use.

Use a solar water heater or preheater.

When repainting building exterior and roof, choose light colors to reflect more sunlight.

Build a roof garden.

LIGHTING

Install lighting with automatic sleep modes and timers. Maintain them.

Replace T-12 fluorescent lighting with energy-efficient T-8 or T-5 LED fixtures.

Replace incandescent bulbs with energy-efficient fluorescents, or better LED lighting.

Increase lighting efficiency by installing optical reflectors and/or diffusers.

Use lighting controls such as dual-technology occupancy sensors, bypass/delay timers, photocells, or time clocks especially in low-occupancy areas.

Properly set and maintain lighting control devices such as time clocks, photocells, and sensors, and adjust for season.

Use task lighting instead of lighting the entire area.

Require janitors or security guards to turn off lights at night. (They don't deter crime.)

Use dimmable ballasts and daylight controls such as astronomical clocks to dim lights to take advantage of daylight. Use timer controls for outside lighting.

Clean lighting fixtures, diffusers, and lamps so they light as effectively as possible (dirt can reduce lighting efficiency by up to 50 percent).

WATER REDUCTION

Work with your water company to develop a site-specific "water budget."

Monitor water bills for spikes in use. Maintenance may be required.

Post clean-up policies, including water-saving plans.

INDOOR USE

Install low-flow toilets, urinals, faucets, and showerheads.

Regularly check for and repair all leaks in your facility. Leaks in toilet tanks can be detected with leak-detecting tablets, which may be available from your water company. A faucet with a slow leak can waste 10 gallons of water a day, or more. A single leaky toilet can waste as much as 1,000 gallons of water per day.

Install low-flow aerators and showerheads (your water company may offer these for free): as low as 0.5 gpm and no greater than 2.5 gpm for lavatory sinks; 2.0 gpm or less for kitchen sinks; 1.0 gpm or less for showerheads.

- Install 1.3 gpf high-efficiency toilets.

- Install waterless urinals.

- Install self-closing faucets (0.5 gpm and 0.25 gallons/cycle).

- Use dry floor-cleaning methods, followed by damp mopping, rather than spraying or hosing with water.

- Change window-cleaning schedule from "periodic" to "as required."

- Reduce water pressure to no higher than 50 psi by installing pressure-reducing valves.

- Replace water-cooled equipment, such as air-conditioning units, with air-cooled equipment or a geothermal heat pump.

OUTDOOR USE

- Irrigate with low-volume, recoverable systems.

- Harvest rainwater.

- Irrigate with gray water (from domestic activities such as laundry and bathing) that contains no animal or human waste.

- Install a self-adjusting, weather-based irrigation controller that automatically tailors watering schedules to match local weather, plant types, and other site-specific conditions.

- Install matched precipitation-rate sprinkler heads for even distribution of water over a surface area. Avoid runoff onto pavement.

- Modify your existing irrigation system to include drip irrigation.

- Install water-flow meters on all large irrigation systems.

- Adjust the irrigation schedule monthly during irrigation season, or as needed.

- Test irrigation sprinklers four times per year to ensure proper operation and coverage; repair all broken or defective sprinkler heads/nozzles, lines, and valves.

- Group plants with similar water requirements together on the same irrigation line.

- Install rain shut-off devices that turn off the irrigation system during rain.

- Reduce irrigation system water pressure to no higher than 50 psi (pressure-reducing valves must be installed to do this).

- Water during pre-dawn hours to reduce water loss from evaporation.

- If installing new turf, limit the area and use drought-tolerant species in low-rain regions. Use repeat cycles when watering turf, planting strips, or shrubs to encourage percolation and deep root growth.

- Use only dry methods to clean outdoor hard surfaces and post instructions for staff.

- When repaving parking lots, install permeable concrete or create berms to drain or direct water into plantings.

WASTE REDUCTION

☐ Target zero waste to the landfill or incinerator.

☐ Centralize purchasing to eliminate waste and ensure that environmental guidelines are followed.

☐ Create signage in the major local languages to specify what can and cannot be thrown in the dumpster.

☐ Check the dumpster periodically to see if what's thrown in belongs there.

☐ Recycle all cardboard, paper, plastic, glass, and metal.

TOXICS REDUCTION

☐ Require the use of low-toxicity cleaning and janitorial products.

☐ Reduce use of chemicals (process chemicals, cleaners, pesticides, paints, etc.).

☐ Crosscheck Material Safety Data Sheets (MSDS) and labels for all chemicals, cleaning products, building maintenance materials, pesticides, and fertilizers you use. Identify safer alternatives. Avoid products with labels containing toxic or carcinogenic content.

☐ Dispose of any hazardous waste at a hazardous-waste center. Recycle universal wastes (spent fluorescent light tubes and bulbs; electronic equipment; and batteries) as required by law.

☐ Store any potentially hazardous materials securely, control access, and rotate stock to use oldest material first.

Seal basement floors with an impermeable coating.

Design berms, secondary containment, or grading to prevent run-off or rain water from flowing across industrial and hazardous liquid storage areas where it could become contaminated.

Place all potential pollutants far away from food-storage areas, as well as from sewer and storm drains.

Routinely check for and address leaks, spills, and emissions of chemicals, paints, and cleaners.

Use an enclosed delivery system, such as pipes or hoses, for transferring cleaners or other chemicals to prevent spills and splashes.

Keep dumpsters covered, not overflowing, and impermeable to rainwater.

Do not wash cars or equipment or other items outside where runoff water flows to the storm drain; this wash water should be directed to a sewer drain.

Post signs at targeted trouble spots to explain how to prevent pollutants from reaching storm drains.

Mulch, or use ground cover, in landscaped areas to prevent exposed soil from washing into storm drains.

Regularly check and maintain storm drain openings and basins. Keep litter, debris, and soil away from storm drains.

Clean private catch basins annually, before the first rain and as needed thereafter.

- Use shut-off valves at storm drains or keep temporary storm-drain plugs available at loading docks or other outdoor staging areas for quick spill response.

- Keep a spill kit handy to catch/collect spills from leaking company or employee vehicles.

- Keep at hand adequate absorbent material to contain the largest possible spill.

- Eliminate the routine use of all disinfectants and sanitizers, unless needed to comply with environmental health codes.

- Use no products with added antibacterial agents, such as triclosan. This includes products for hand washing, dishwashing, and cleaning.

- Reduce or replace disinfectants used in industrial processes with environmentally preferable products.

- Eliminate or reduce pesticides by using Integrated Pest Management (IPM), which includes good housekeeping, acting only when needed, making physical changes to keep pests out, and, lastly, using fewer or nontoxic pesticides.

- Keep kitchen, waste storage, and other areas clean to prevent pest problems.

- When pest control is necessary, use barriers (such as caulking/sealing holes), traps, and lastly, less toxic pesticides (such as soaps, oils, microbials and baits). Apply only as needed (rather than on a routine schedule).

If you contract with a pest-control operator, choose one that is EcoWise Certified (ecowisecertified.com), or specify in the contract with a conventional operator the use of IPM and nonchemical pest-prevention and pest-exclusion methods.

Do not allow outdoor perimeter spraying.

Purchase organically or locally grown foods and beverages for the lunchroom or café.

Use low- or no-VOC paint products.

Use high-efficiency paint spray equipment with high-solids (low-solvent) paint.

Use natural or low-emissions building materials, carpets, or furniture.

{ 119 }

Replace standard fluorescent lights with no-mercury LED lights.

Obtain a battery recharger for the office. Use rechargeable (instead of disposable) batteries for flashlights, radios, remote controls, and other devices.

Use recycled oil for vehicles/equipment.

Use unbleached and/or chlorine-free paper products (copy paper, paper towels, napkins, coffee filters, etc.).

Print promotional materials with vegetable or other low-VOC inks.

- If hazardous materials are essential to your product and cannot be eliminated, design it so that that these materials can be extracted and recycled into new products.

- Develop a consumer take-back system (e.g., for printer cartridges) to recover spent products.

- Place into appropriate waste containers used copier toner and ink-jet cartridges, as well as car fluids from company vehicles.

- Donate out-of-date but still functioning electronic equipment for reuse.

CONSTRUCTION TIPS

- LEED-certify all construction activities for your facilities.

- Recycle what you can from demolition, including wood, wallboard, and carpeting.

- Specify recycled content for carpet and backing, lumber/ wood, cabinets, fixtures, drywall, partitions, ceramic and ceiling tiles, roofing, and concrete.

- Rearrange workspaces to take advantage of areas with natural light and design for increased natural lighting when remodeling.

OFFICE TIPS

- Specify recycled materials whenever they meet performance standards. These include cardboard, paper (envelopes, letterhead, business cards, paper towels, tissue, toilet paper, and seat covers), garbage bags, and laser and copier toner cartridges.

Use Energy Star copiers and fax machines: they have lower annual electricity costs of about 60 percent and 50 percent respectively. Energy Star-compliant monitors have power-management features and consume up to 90 percent less energy.

Use power-management software programs to automatically turn off computers and printers.

Use the standby mode on equipment (e.g., energy saver buttons on copiers).

Discourage the printing of e-mails.

Ensure that copier/printer paper is at least 30 percent recycled.

Set copier defaults to double-sided.

Use fax modems that permit faxing without printing.

Eliminate fax cover sheets.

Eliminate unnecessary forms; redesign forms to use less paper; switch to electronic forms.

Reduce junk mail and eliminate duplicates of mailings you want to receive. To obtain guidance, go to www.stopjunkmail.org or www.catalogchoice.org.

Subscribe to journals online.

Minimize the use of physical manuals; use them online.

- Use a bulletin board or routing slips to reduce the number of printed copies.

- Eliminate duplicates in your own mailing lists.

- Use soy-based or low-VOC inks.

- Lease rather than purchase computers and printers.

- Print on previously printed paper for drafts (designate a draft tray).

- Create a reuse area for office supplies such as used envelopes, binders, and folders.

- Have toner cartridges refilled.

- Analyze paper use by department; work with big consumers on paperless alternatives.

LUNCHROOM OR CAFÉ TIPS

- Eliminate the use of nonrecyclable packaging in the lunchroom or café; replace disposables with permanent mugs, dishes, utensils, towels/rags, coffee filters, etc; avoid the use of individual condiments packets.

- Use Energy Star refrigerators.

- Serve dishes at office events in reusable serving dishes.

- Eliminate the use of single-serving disposable water bottles.

- Compost kitchen waste.

LANDSCAPING TIPS

Do not use leaf blowers: they blow particulates around, as well as leaves; gas-powered leaf blowers cause air as well as noise pollution.

Leave mowed grass on the lawn for "green-cycling."

In dry regions, avoid lawns in favor of xeriscape.

RETAIL STORE TIP

Provide, or sell at cost, cloth instead of paper bags; eliminate or reduce packaging.

THE RESPONSIBLE COMPANY

ACKNOWLEDGMENTS

FIRST THANKS GO TO Michael Brown, Patagonia's first environmental director, who now runs his own consultancy (Brown & Wilmanns Environmental, www.bw-environmental.com). An early vision of this book grew out of a year of breakfast talks between Vincent and Mike. Jill Dumain, Mike's successor and Patagonia's current director of environmental strategy, has lent her watchful eye and quick mind to several drafts of the manuscript and has been an invaluable partner in the work. Special thanks go to Patagonia board member Charles Conn, a committed and critical reader of the original manuscript.

Writers usually can only dream of having an editor as engaged, unflinching, good humored, and devoted to her work as Susan Bell. We were lucky to find her (thanks to Ira Silverberg) and honored to have her on the case, as the reader's best friend and authors' guardian angel, from the first revision through the last. Susan introduced us to Barbara deWilde, who turned our typescript into the book in your hands. Thanks to Geoffrey Ravenhill for the notes and the index, and to Carly Berwick and Natalie Spolyar, proofreaders. Thanks also to Sterling Lord agents Flip Brophy and Szilvia Molnar; Larry Gadd of North River Press for his counsel; CamelBak CEO Sally McCoy for her thoughtful reading; Jen Rapp, Patagonia's PR ace; and Jennifer Sullivan, our production shepherd.

{ 125 }

Thanks to the other members of the Patagonia book team: John Dutton, Rick Ridgeway, Annette Scheid, Jane Sievert, and Christina Speed; to Footprinters Stuart Bjornlie, Alyssa Firmin, Jim Little, Elissa Loughman, Lisa Polley, and Eric Unmacht; to the company's editorial team including the late Mike Colpo, Diane French, Craig Holloway, Kasey Kersnowski, Carin Knutson, and Betsy Manninen; to Rob BonDurant and Megan Marble; to Mike Dunn; and to those unnamed who have given, or will give, their time and thought to this project. Its shortcomings are the authors'.

Last to be named, first always: Malinda Chouinard and Nora Gallagher, our respective mates in love, life, and work. Thanks every day, for every day.

ACKNOWLEDGMENTS

THE RESPONSIBLE COMPANY

RECOMMENDED READING

BROWN, LESTER R. *World on the Edge*
(New York: W.W. Norton, 2011)

CHOUINARD, YVON. *Let My People Go Surfing*
(New York: Penguin, 2006)

EASTY, DANIEL C. AND ANDREW S. WINSTON. *Green to Gold*
(New Haven: Yale University Press, 2006)

GOLEMAN, DANIEL. *Ecological Intelligence*
(New York: Broadway Books, 2009)

GUNTHER, MARC. *Faith and Fortune*
(New York: Crown Business, 2004)

HAWKEN, PAUL. *The Ecology of Commerce* Revised edition
(New York: Collins Business Essentials, 2010)

HAWKEN, PAUL, AMORY LOVINS, L. HUNTER LOVINS.
Natural Capitalism (New York: Little, Brown, 1999)

HUMES, EDWARD. *Force of Nature*
(New York: Harper Business, 2011)

MCDONOUGH, WILLIAM AND MICHAEL BRAUNGART. *Cradle to Cradle*
(New York: North Point, 2002)

MCKIBBEN, BILL. *Deep Economy*
(New York: Times Books, 2007)

STACK, JACK AND BO BURLINGHAM. *A Stake in the Outcome*
(New York: Doubleday Business, 2002)

CHAPTER 1: WHAT WE DO FOR A LIVING

The Economist noted in his obituary: "The Carpet-tile philosopher: Ray Anderson, America's greenest businessman, died on August 8th, aged 77," *The Economist*, September 10, 2011, www.economist.com/node/21528583.

Jack Stack, who with other employees had bought back the failing Springfield Remanufacturing Company from International Harvester: Bo Burlingham, "America's 25 Most Fascinating Entrepreneurs: Jack Stack, SRC Holdings," *INC. Magazine*, 2004, www.inc.com /magazine/20040401/25stack.html. {131}

Google allows employees to spend 20 percent of their working time doing almost anything they like: Google Inc., "The Engineer's Life at Google," 2011, www.google.com/intl/en/jobs/lifeatgoogle/englife /index.html.

one or more of 400 new indexes to benchmark: "Ecolabel Index is the largest global directory of ecolabels;" Ecolabel Index, home page, accessed March 10, 2012, www.ecolabelindex.com.

Every company should be afraid, as is Wal-Mart, of teenagers: Edward Humes, *Force of Nature* (New York: HarperCollins, 2011), 235.

54 percent of customers thought Wal-Mart "too aggressive," 82 percent expected the company to be a "role model for other businesses," and 2 to 8 percent, as many as fourteen million people, had stopped shopping

at Wal-Mart altogether: Edward Humes, *Force of Nature* (New York: HarperCollins, 2011), 52.

According to a new Harvard Business School study, socially responsible investments, which once underperformed more exciting opportunities like subprime mortgages, now over the long term outperform the market as a whole: Robert G. Eccles, Ioannis Ioannou, and George Serafeim, "The Impact of a Corporate Culture of Sustainability on Corporate Behavior and Performance," (Harvard Business School Working Paper, No. 12-035, November 2011).

Nike, stung by public disgust over child labor in its contract factories: "Nike & Responsibility: A Look into the Future," University of Delaware Department of Fashion and Apparel Studies, FIBER, 2008, www.udel.edu /fiber/issue1/responsibility/.

Coca-Cola has committed to return its wastewater to the environment clean enough "to support aquatic life and agriculture.": Brian Walsh, "Paying for Nature," *Time Magazine*, Februay 21, 2011, www.time.com/time /magazine/article/0,9171,2048324,00.html.

{ 132 }

Dow has recently teamed with The Nature Conservancy: John Flesher, "Dow, Nature Conservancy pledge cooperation," *Bloomberg BusinessWeek*, January 24, 2011, www.businessweek.com/ap/financialnews/D9KV0EA81.htm.

Both Coca-Cola and Dow have teamed with Kellogg's, DuPont, and others to develop "material-neutral" packaging: Rachel Cernansky, "Coca Cola, DuPont, Kellogg's and Others Establish a Trade Organization for Sustainable Packaging," *Tree Hugger*, March 10, 2011, www.treehugger.com /files/2011/03/coca-cola-dupont-kelloggs-establish-trade-organization-sustainable-packaging.php.

Wal-Mart, the world's largest company, formerly committed to an exclusive strategy of low prices, regardless of environmental cost, has committed to use 100 percent renewable energy, create zero waste, and to "sell products that sustain our resources and environment.": Edward Humes, *Force of Nature* (New York: HarperCollins, 2011), 104.

the Prius is succeeding the late Crown Victoria as the emblematic tax-exempt fleet vehicle: Responsible Purchasing Network, "Responsible Purchasing Guide: Light-Duty Fleet Vehicles," 2007, www.seattle.gov /purchasing/pdf/RPNFleets.pdf.

The conservative but troubled U.S. dairy industry is now engaged in large-scale projects to increase the productivity and shelf life of milk without resorting to destructive factory-farm practices; to change cattle feed to reduce methane "burps" (a significant contributor to greenhouse gases); and to harvest cow patties for use as organic fertilizer: Edward Humes, *Force of Nature* (New York: HarperCollins, 2011), 162-180.

Enter the LEED certification system for building to energy-efficient standards with less environmental harm. At the time it was introduced in 2000, only 635 buildings worldwide could comply. As of 2012, more than 40,000 LEED-certified projects have been built or are in the works: Daniel Goleman, *Ecological Intelligence* (New York: Broadway Books, 2009), 136.

A LEED retrofit saves owners an annual 90 cents a square foot; they make their investment back in two years: Amy Cortese, "'Green' Buildings Don't Have to Be New," *The New York Times*, January 27, 2008, www.nytimes.com /2008/01/27/realestate/commercial/27sqft.html?scp=1&sq=LEED retrofit.

low-income housing built by developer Jonathan Rose: Jonathan Rose Companies, www.rose-network.com/green-urban-solutions-landing /green-urban-solutions; Vivian Marino, "Square Feet/The Interview;" *The New York Times*, January 17, 2010, www.nytimes.com/2010/01/17 /realestate/17sqft.html?_r=183&scp=2&sq=Jonathan Rose&st=cse

They benefited from participation by Nike, which had invested seven years of work and $6 million to create its Environmental Apparel Design Tool: Tilde Herrera, "Eco-Index apparel tool gets an upgrade, moves to pilot phase," *Business Green*, August 23, 2011, www.businessgreen.com/ bg/news/2103668/eco-index-apparel-tool-upgrade-moves-pilot-phase. See Berkeley professor Dara O'Rourke's Good Guide rating system: GoodGuide, www.goodguide.com/about.

As a result, the much larger Sustainable Apparel Coalition, whose members produce more than 30 percent of the clothing and footwear sold globally, will benefit from the OIA's work: Yvon Chouinard, Jib Ellison, Rick Ridgeway, "The Big Idea: The Sustainable Economy." *Harvard Business Review*, (October 2011): 59; http://hbr.org/2011/10/the-sustainable -economy/ar/1.

Yvon and John Fleming, Wal-Mart's Chief Merchandising Officer, co-signed an invitation written on joint letterhead to attend the "21st Century Apparel Leadership Consortium": Yvon Chouinard, John Fleming, "21st Century Apparel Leadership Consortium," invitation letter, January 10, 2009.

The invitees agreed to become the Sustainable Apparel Coalition: Yvon Chouinard, Jib Ellison, Rick Ridgeway, "The Big Idea: The Sustainable Economy." *Harvard Business Review*, (October 2011): 59; http://hbr. org/2011/10/the-sustainable-economy/ar/1.

Similar efforts are underway in other industries, with over 400 indexes in effect or being considered: Ecolabel Index, accessed March 10, 2012, www.ecolabelindex.com.

As Wal-Mart has discovered, 90 percent of a product's environmental impact is determined at the design stage: Daniel Goleman, *Ecological Intelligence* (New York: Broadway Books, 2009), 93.

Closer to home: a Patagonia polo shirt is made of organic cotton from an irrigated field, whose cultivation requires nearly 2,700 liters of water, enough to meet the daily needs (three glasses a day) of 900 people. Each polo shirt, in its journey from the cotton field to our Reno warehouse, generates nearly 21 pounds of carbon dioxide, 30 times the weight of the finished product. Along the line, it generates three times its weight in waste: Patagonia Inc., "Polo Shirt," *Footprint Chronicles*, accessed December 28, 2011, www.patagonia.com/us/footprint.

CHAPTER 2: WHAT CRISIS?
The philosopher Alfred North Whitehead described how we experience
nature's "creative advance" as perpetual novelty. But nature generates its
changes at a much slower pace than we now allow her: Alfred North
Whitehead, *The Concept of Nature* (Cambridge: Cambridge University Press,
1920); 178.

The EPA identified 62,000 industrial chemicals in 1979, without
screening or proscribing their use. Only a few hundred have even been
tested. You carry in your own body traces of 200 chemicals unknown to
your ancestors, some of them toxic in large amounts, others slow-acting
carcinogens in small amounts. And a chemical present in your blood
might have no affect on its own, but prove dangerous in combination
with another. Untested interactions among the various chemicals
released into nature can form up to three billion combinations: Daniel
Goleman, *Ecological Intelligence* (New York: Broadway Books, 2009), 153.

These include inflammatory autoimmune disorders like asthma, allergies, lupus, and multiple sclerosis. Nonsmokers who reach middle age
can now expect to have levels of chronic obstructive pulmonary disease
(COPD), a precursor to emphysema, equal to that of smokers: Daniel
Goleman, *Ecological Intelligence* (New York: Broadway Books, 2009), 152.

Breast cancer rates: M. H. Forouzanfar et. al., "Breast and cervical cancer in
187 countries between 1980 and 2010: a systematic analysis," *Lancet* 378, no.
9801 (October 2011): 1461-1484. www.ncbi.nlm.nih.gov/pubmed/21924486.

We have added significantly, through runoff from sewage and fertilizer,
to the nitrogen and phosphorus in the water supply; the extra nutrients
create algae blooms that choke off oxygen and kill fish. Half of the lakes
in Asia, Europe, and North America suffer from this process, called
eutrophication, as does much of the Gulf of Mexico: Daniel Goleman,
Ecological Intelligence (New York: Broadway Books, 2009), 58.

The atmospheric concentration of carbon dioxide, up by 19 percent since 1959, has now reached its highest level in 600,000 years and continues to grow, making hot air hotter, cold air colder, and increasing the ferocity of storms. Arctic winter ice decreases nine percent each decade and every winter more of western Antarctica's ice shelves calve into the ocean: NASA, "Global Climate Change," www.climate.nasa.gov.

Larsen B Ice Shelf: NASA, "Researchers Provide Detailed Picture of Ice Loss Following Collapse of Antarctic Ice Shelves," July 25, 2011, www.nasa.gov /topics/earth/features/larsen-collapse.html.

In 1960, humanity consumed about half of the planet's potential resource capacity. By 1987, we exceeded it. Twenty-five years later we are using the resources of one and a half planets, though the pattern of consumption is unequal. Europe, proportionate to its population, consumes the equivalent resources of three planets; North Americans, seven. The consumers are unevenly distributed, and so is the consumption, though China and India, the world's most populous countries, now have sizeable, growing, appetitive middle classes: World Wildlife Fund, "Living Planet Report 2010: A Summary," 2010, p. 13, wwf.panda.org /about_our_earth/all_publications/living_planet_report/2010_lpr/.

Biologists agree that we're in the midst of the planet's sixth extinction crisis (the fifth was that of the dinosaurs). A 2009 study in Nature named biodiversity as the "planetary boundary" that humans have violated more than any other, among nine identified "Earth-system processes and associated thresholds, which, if crossed, could generate unacceptable environmental change." Their proposed threshold for extinction was ten species per million per year. We are losing species now at the rate of 100 per million per year, or 1,000 times (not a typo) the normal rate. Thirty percent of amphibians and 21 percent of mammals are among the most imminently vulnerable, including the polar bear, rhinoceros, tiger, giraffe and gorilla. Twelve percent of bird species are threatened with extinction, as are 73 percent of flowering plants, 27 percent of corals, and 50 percent of fungi and protists:

John Mulrow, "World Will Completely Miss 2010 Biodiversity Target," *Vital Signs 2011*, (Washington DC: Worldwatch Institute, 2011), 40.

Water withdrawals from lakes and rivers have doubled since 1960. As more of the earth's major rivers—on which huge populations depend— fail to reach the sea, the ocean's coastal eutrophic, or dead, zones expand. The dammed Colorado River is now rarely allowed to flow into the Gulf of Mexico and its former delta is a toxic swamp. By 2025, no Chinese river will meet the ocean all year long: "Current State & Trends Assessment Report," Millennium Ecosystem Assessment, 2005, www.maweb.org/en/Condition.aspx.

at the rate of one inch a year in the American Midwest. It takes 500 years for an inch of topsoil to form naturally: "Why Do You Need to Care about Kansas Soil," U.S. Dept. of Agriculture, Natural Resources Conservation Service, www.ks.nrcs.usda.gov/soils/stsoil.html.

Richard Nixon, on signing the Endangered Species Act, said: Richard Nixon, "Special Message to the Congress Outlining the 1972 Environmental Program," February 8, 1972, www.presidency.ucsb.edu/ws /index.php?pid=3731#axzz1ZXhtAyP5.

The respected Environmental Performance Index (EPI) in 2010 ranked the world's five top countries as Iceland, Switzerland, Costa Rica, Sweden, and Norway. Germany, the U. K. France, and Japan are all in the top 20. The U.S. has fallen to the sixty-first position: Environmental Performance Index: 2010, www.wikipedia.org/Environmental_ Performance_Index; www.epi.yale.edu.

This decline reflects Americans' growing environmental apathy. In a 2011 poll, Pew Research Center reported that only 40 percent of Americans considered protecting the environment a high priority, down from 63 percent ten years earlier: Pew Research Center, "Economy Dominates Public's Agenda, Dims Hopes for the Future: Public's Policy Priorities," January 20th, 2011, http://people-press.org/2011/01/20 /section-1-publics-policy-priorities/.

It would take, if it were possible, the muscle power of 700,000 people to power the flight of a jet: Thomas J. Plocek, Offshore Infrastructure Associates, Inc., "Power and Economic Development," April 24, 2008.

More than a billion people now live in areas threatened by desertification: The United Nations Convention to Combat Desertification, www.un.org/ecosocdev/geninfo/sustdev/desert.htm.

In the U.S., according to one researcher, five out of six lost manufacturing jobs could be attributed to increased productivity (with the remaining one of six jobs lost to offshoring and other causes): W. A. Ward, "Manufacturing Jobs, 2000-2005," *Economic Development Journal 5* (Winter 2006) (1): 7-15.

In 2011, Puma commissioned PriceWaterhouseCoopers to help develop an "Environmental Profit and Loss" statement to account for the full impact of the brand on ecosystems. The consultancy firm hopes to create a model robust enough to be adopted by other companies: Yvon Chouinard, Jib Ellison, Rick Ridgeway, "The Big Idea: The Sustainable Economy." *Harvard Business Review,* (October 2011): 59; http://hbr.org/2011/10/the-sustainable-economy/ar/1.

{ 138 }

In 2010, Robert Zoellick, president of the World Bank, announced a major project to work with emerging and developing countries to quantify their natural capital, roughly estimated at a value of $44 trillion worldwide: Andrew Revkin, "World Bank Pushes to Include Ecology in Accounting," *The New York Times,* October 28, 2010, Opinion Pages, http://dotearth.blogs.nytimes.com/2010/10/28/world-bank-pushes-to-include-ecology-in-accounting/?scp=2&sq=10/28/10%20world%20bank&st=cse.

An organization called B Labs grants "B Corporation" accreditation to companies that meet its standards: The B Lab, "B Corporations," www.bcorporation.net.

And broad, innovative applications of those 400-plus social and

environmental indexes will help customers choose products made by companies that pay fairly and work to tangibly reduce their environmental damage: Ecolabel Index is the largest global directory of ecolabels, Ecolabel Index, 2011, www.ecolabelindex.com.

Companies, not individuals, generate 75 percent of the trash that reaches the landfill or incinerator: Annie Leonard, *The Story of Stuff* (New York: Free Press, 2010), 295.

Germany, Japan, and China, among other governments, have announced their intention to create "circular economies" that promote reduction, reuse, and recycling of materials. Japan passed a law in 2000 to increase resource productivity by 60 percent and recycling by 40 to 50 percent, and to reduce waste disposal by 60 percent by 2010. As of 2008, it was on track, according to World Watch's 2011 report: Gary Gardner, "Global Output Stagnant," *Vital Signs 2011* (Washington DC: Worldwatch Institute, 2011), 75.

The U.S. Treasury, for example, pays $2 billion a year to support the price of chemically intensive conventional cotton grown in California and Texas: Missy Ryan, "U.S. is expected to lose WTO fight on cotton subsidies," *The New York Times*, February 14, 2008, www.nytimes.com /2008/02/14/business/worldbusiness/14iht-cotton.1.10040057.html.

as economist Joseph Stiglitz puts it, we need to expand the idea of GDP to include noneconomic factors: Joseph E. Stiglitz, Amartya Sen, and Jean-Paul Fitoussi, *Mismeasuring Our Lives: Why GDP Doesn't Add Up* (New York: The News Press, 2010).

In October 2010, the U. K., following the lead of Bhutan, Canada, and France, adopted (with some nervousness on the part of its Conservative government) a "happiness index" that defines quality of life more broadly than does GDP: Allegra Stratton, "David Cameron aims to make happiness the new GDP," *The Guardian*, November 14, 2010, www.guardian.co.uk /politics/2010/nov/14/david-cameron-wellbeing-inquiry.

Not in the U.S., where it has been illegal to make land mines since 1997, but offshore, through its supply chain. Land mines hurt mostly civilians: 158 countries (the U.S. not included) have called for an international ban: International Campaign to Ban Landmines, press release, www.icbl.org /index.php/icbl/Library/News-Articles/Universal/pr-25Nov09.

Science journalist Daniel Goleman in *Ecological Intelligence* offered three simple, yet remarkably comprehensive rules for reducing environmental harm: "Know your impacts, favor improvement, share what you learn." This applies to us all, in large and small companies, as we begin to, or continue to, act: Daniel Goleman, *Ecological Intelligence* (New York: Broadway Books, 2009), 50.

CHAPTER 4: MEANINGFUL WORK
There is a word for it, and the word is clean. Climbing with only nuts and runners for protection is clean climbing. Clean because the rock is left unaltered by the passing climber. Clean because nothing is hammered into the rock and then hammered back out, leaving the rock scarred and the next climber's experience less natural. Clean because the climber's protection leaves little trace of his ascension. Clean is climbing the rock without changing it; a step closer to organic climbing for the natural man: Doug Robinson, "The Whole Natural Art of Protection," *Chouinard Equipment Catalog*, 1972, 12.

{ 140 }

1% for the Planet: see www.onepercentfortheplanet.org.

The Environmental Protection Agency (EPA) would acknowledge these dangers two decades later when Hurricane Katrina victims got sick from the formaldehyde in their FEMA trailers: National Academy of Sciences, "EPA's Draft Health Assessment for Formaldehyde Needs Improvement," April 8, 2011, www.nationalacademies.org/onpinews /newsitem.aspx?RecordID=13142.

To prepare soil for planting cotton, workers spray organophosphates (which can damage the human central nervous system) to kill off all other living organisms. The soil, once treated, is doornail dead (five pesticide-free years have to pass before earthworms, an indication of soil health, can return). Such soil requires intensive use of artificial fertilizers to mechanically hold the cotton plants in place. Rainwater runoff from cotton fields contributes significantly to the growth of ocean dead zones: Edward Humes, *Force of Nature* (New York: HarperCollins, 2011), 126.

Cotton fields, representing 2.5 percent of cultivated land, ingest 15 percent of chemical insecticides used in agriculture and 10 percent of pesticides. About one tenth of one percent of these chemicals reach the pests they target: Edward Humes, *Force of Nature* (New York: HarperCollins, 2011): 126.

Genetically modified Bt (*Bacillus thuringiensis*) cotton, introduced in the past decade, reduces pesticide use initially by more specifically targeting leaf-eating bollworms. China, which planted Bt cotton on a large scale in the early 2000s, found that after a few seasons, grass bugs and other pests immune to Bt stepped into the breach left by the bollworms; wholesale spraying had to be resumed: Guillaume Gruère, Purvi Mehta-Bhatt, Debdatta Sengupta, "Bt Cotton and farmer suicides in India," International Food Policy Research Institute Discussion Paper 00808, 2008, www.ifpri.org/publication/bt-cotton-and-farmer-suicides-india. { 141 }

Cotton fields contribute 165 million metric tons of greenhouse gas emissions every year: Edward Humes, *Force of Nature* (New York: HarperCollins, 2011), 126-27.

Before harvesting in non-frost regions like California, cotton has to be sprayed by a cropduster with the defoliant Paraquat, about half of which hits its target. The rest settles over the neighbors' fields and into our streams: Daniel Goleman, *Ecological Intelligence* (New York: Broadway Books, 2009), 23.

We've learned since what textiles do to water. You can now see, on Google Earth satellite images, the pollution of the Pearl River where it flows indigo into the South China Sea. Indigo is the color of the discharge from the world's major jeans factories upstream in Xingtang: Emily Chang, "China's famed Pearl River under denim threat," CNN World, April 26, 2010, www.articles.cnn.com/2010-04-26/world/china.denim .water.pollution_1_denim-pearl-river-factory?_s=PM:WORLD.

The World Bank estimates nearly 20 percent of industrial water pollution comes from textile dyeing and treatment. They've also identified seventy-two toxic chemicals in our water that have textile dyes as their source; these dyes, when not controlled in the workplace, can compromise the health of employees: Samuel Hong Shen Chan, Ta Yeong Wu, Joon Ching Juan, Chee Yang The, "Recent developments of metal oxide semiconductors as photocatalysts in advanced oxidation processes (AOPs) for treatment of dye waste-water," *Journal of Chemical Technology and Biotechnology* 86, no. 9 (September 2011): 1130-58, http://onlinelibrary.wiley.com /doi/10.1002/jctb.2636/abstract.

In 2010, both China and India closed textile mills on a vast scale for violation of pollution laws. In Madras, the government required the local power company to discontinue service to 700 mills until they complied with the law: Aaron Raybin, "Excessive water pollution closes Indian dye houses," AirDye Inc., May 2, 2011, http://blog.airdye.com /goodforbusiness/2011/05/02 excessive-water-pollution-closes-indian -dye-houses/.

fifteen years from now, between one-third and one-half of the world's population will live in an area famished by drought: Global Warming Forecasts: 2025, www.global-warming-forecasts.com/2025-climate -change-global-warming-2025.php.

"Your customers," said owner Jef Stokes, "have a right to know if their jacket was sewn by a 12-year-old girl working all day for a bowl of rice.": Patagonia Inc., "What Is Quality for Our Time?" *Footprint Chronicles* Video, www.video.patagonia.com/video What-is-Quality-for-Our-Time-Re.

According to the view of psychologist Abraham Maslow, however, our family members had yet to meet the two highest, most complex requirements in his hierarchy of needs: a sense of worth and self-fulfillment. It was Maslow's view that needs must be met in the order of their importance for survival: basics first, self-fulfillment last: A.H. Maslow, "A Theory of Human Motivation," *Psychological Review* 50, (1943), 370-96.

Yet when a labor-rights group revealed that Kathie Lee Gifford's clothing line for Wal-Mart was sewn by 12-year-olds, we wondered whether we were doing anything close: The National Labor Committee, "Children Found Sewing Clothing For Wal-Mart, Hanes & Other U.S. & European Companies," Harvard Law School, www.law.harvard.edu/programs/lwp /NLC_childlabor.html.

Out of this task force came the Fair Labor Association (FLA), an independent nonprofit monitoring organization dedicated to fair pay and decent working conditions: Fair Labor Association, www.fairlabor.org.

We began to consider the cradle-to-cradle thinking of architect William McDonough, who believes that just as natural waste regenerates life, human-made products at the end of their time should be remade into new products, preferably of equal value: William McDonough and Michael Braungart, *Cradle to Cradle: Remaking the Way We Make Things* (New York: North Point Press, 2002).

{ 143 }

CHAPTER 5: THE ELEMENTS OF BUSINESS RESPONSIBILITY
The best answer is to follow Daniel Goleman's creed: Know your impacts, favor improvement, share what you learn: Daniel Goleman, *Ecological Intelligence* (New York: Broadway Books, 2009).

In 1994, consultant John Elkington coined the phrase "triple bottom line" (TBL), which measures indicators of social health (defined as human capital) and the planet (natural capital) as well as profit (capital). In 2007, the United Nations ratified TBL as a standard for public-sector accounting, as a means to measure the true cost of government subsidies to industry: Denise Caruso, "When Balance Sheets Collide With the New Economy," *The New York Times*, September 9, 2007, www.nytimes.com /2007/09/09/business/09frame.html.

Two NGOs, The Nature Conservancy and Conservation International, are working with the accounting firm PriceWaterhouseCoopers to develop new methodologies to valuate ecosystems. As we mentioned in the first chapter, Dow Chemical has committed to invest $10 million over five years in partnership with The Nature Conservancy to

develop strategies to price nature's unpaid work as a provider of
biodiversity and "ecosystem services"; one-third of global food
production, for example, relies on insect and animal pollination:
Yvon Chouinard, Jib Ellison, Rick Ridgeway, "The Big Idea: The
Sustainable Economy." *Harvard Business Review*, (October 2011): 59;
http://hbr.org/2011/10/the-sustainable-economy/ar/1.

This is the idea behind a budding movement called Creating Shared
Value (CSV): Michael Porter, Mark Kramer, "Strategy & Society: The Link
Between Competitive Advantage and Corporate Social Responsibility,"
Harvard Business Review, (December 2006); http://hbr.org/product
/strategy-and-society-the-link-between-competitive-/an
/R0612D-PDF-ENG.

Hard to quarrel with that, or with Robert Zoellick, the president of
the World Bank, who is starting a project to assign a dollar value to
the natural capital of emerging and developing nations, because "the
natural wealth of nations should be a capital asset, valued in combination with its financial capital, manufactured capital, and human
capital.": Andrew Revkin, "World Bank Pushes to Include Ecology in
Accounting," *The New York Times*, October 28, 2010, Opinion Pages,
http://dotearth.blogs.nytimes.com/2010/10/28/world-bank-pushes
-to-include-ecology-in-accounting/.

Anthropologist Robin Dunbar cites 150 as the magic number for
community cohesion, based on the number of human relationships
the human brain can handle. When it builds a new plant, the manufacturer W. L. Gore, puts in 150 parking spaces. When the plant
exceeds that capacity, the company builds a new one. Microsoft and
Intel also a limit the number of employees per building to 150,
though they both run plants with multiple buildings. Hutterites form
a new community when they reach that number. Along the same lines,
a military company comprises between 80 and 225 people: Malcolm
Gladwell, *The Tipping Point* (New York: Back Bay Books, 2002).

The *Wall Street Journal* has reported that income disparity in the United States now approaches that of Mexico or the Philippines. Procter & Gamble, one of the last mass marketers, now has to pitch its products high or low; not enough people are left in the middle to matter: Ellen Byron, "As Middle Class Shrinks, P&G Aims High and Low," *TheWall Street Journal*, September 12, 2011, http://online.wsj.com/article/SB10001424053111904836104576558861943984924.html?KEY WORDS=middle+class+shrinks.

CHAPTER 6: SHARING KNOWLEDGE
When Wal-Mart wanted to make more systematic improvements and implement its goal of 100 percent renewable energy use, zero waste, and products "that sustain our resources and the environment," it went to its suppliers for help: Edward Humes, *Force of Nature* (New York: HarperCollins, 2011), 104.

Wal-Mart had discovered that only 10 percent of its environmental impact came from store operations and transportation, whereas 90 percent lay in the supply chain: Edward Humes, *Force of Nature* (New York: HarperCollins, 2011), 81.

We met with Arvind and said we wanted to discuss this visit on our website and work with them to solve the violations over time. They agreed: Patagonia Inc., "Conspiracy or Transparency?" Footprint Chronicles, 2010, www.thecleanestline.com/2010/09/footprint-chronicles-fall-2010-update.html.

{ 145 }

THE RESPONSIBLE COMPANY

INDEX

{ 148 }

{ 149 }

{ 157 }